# Finding Fatherhood

Benson Saulo

Published by Benson Saulo, 2025.

While every precaution has been taken in the preparation of this book, the publisher assumes no responsibility for errors or omissions, or for damages resulting from the use of the information contained herein.

FINDING FATHERHOOD

**First edition. November 10, 2025.**

Copyright © 2025 Benson Saulo.

ISBN: 978-1764200714

Written by Benson Saulo.

# Table of Contents

Introduction .................................................................. 1

Where's the Blueprint .................................................. 5

Our Shared Experience ............................................. 17

The Starting Point ..................................................... 31

The Balancing Act ..................................................... 43

Facing the Fear .......................................................... 57

Art of Being Present ................................................. 69

The Wisdom Collective ............................................ 87

Rituals that Matter ................................................... 97

Communication is Key .......................................... 105

Building Resilience ................................................ 121

Energy and Focus ................................................... 135

The Next Generation ............................................. 151

Lessons Learned ..................................................... 167

An Ongoing Journey .............................................. 179

A Call to Lead ......................................................... 189

To my family - Kate, Anais, Eli and Maia, thank you for your love, patience and the lessons you continue to teach me.

To all the fathers who shared your honest reflections and candid insights. You reminded me that presence not perfection is the greatest gift we can share with our children.

# Introduction

*"The biggest lesson was that fatherhood isn't a destination, it's a series of moments, choices, and reflections. Hearing that echoed in so many voices helped me realise I wasn't alone in figuring it out as I go."*

I was walking along the St Kilda Beach Esplanade in Melbourne, pushing a pram with my two-year-old son Eli. He was quietly watching the waves roll in, fascinated by seagulls pestering sunbathers, while I was deep in thought, reflecting on the whirlwind of the past twelve months. My young family of four had just returned to Australia after three years living overseas.

During that time, I held a high-pressure role as a diplomat and trade commissioner, stretched across multiple countries and time zones. The job was fulfilling, but it left little room for being fully present with my wife and children.

Within nine months of coming home, we'd moved house again before we had even unpacked the boxes from our last move. We were navigating new daycare centres, settling into a new job, and adjusting to the news that baby number three was on the way. And, just to add to the chaos, I had decided to run for federal office in the upcoming election. Life wasn't slowing down. It was accelerating.

As the weight of it all settled on me during that walk, a simple thought surfaced: How are other dads doing this? How are they balancing the demands of work, life, ambition, and fatherhood? That question brought me back to my own upbringing. I wondered whether my dad carried similar pressures, whether his idea of being a provider was as all-consuming as it sometimes feels for me. That question lit a spark.

I began reaching out to men I admired: entrepreneurs, executives, grassroots leaders, many of whom were in the same season of life: raising young children. What started as a single conversation with a friend became dozens of honest, vulnerable interviews with fathers navigating the messiness and beauty of modern parenting.

*Finding Fatherhood* isn't a rulebook. It's not a guide to perfect parenting. It's the book I wish I had when I became a father. It's a space for shared stories and real reflections from dads doing their best to juggle ambition, identity, and raising a family.

Through these conversations, I learned new ways to be present after long days, to pause and celebrate the small wins, and to better understand the mental load carried by my partner.

Fatherhood is deeply personal, but we all walk some common ground. We want to raise our children with love, stability, and purpose. We want to show up, even when we're stretched thin.

What I hope you take away from *Finding Fatherhood* is that you are not alone in the tension you might feel between being a present father, a professional, a partner or a friend. This book was born from a deeply personal question "how are other fathers doing this?" and it became a shared journey of learning, honesty, and reflection.

Every conversation that shaped this book reveals that fatherhood is not a puzzle to be solved but an evolving process. The doubt, the pressure, the joy, and more... It's all part of the journey.

My hope for anyone who picks up this book is that they feel less isolated in their challenges, more seen in their efforts, and more confident in their capabilities.

*Finding Fatherhood* seeks to spark reflection, conversation, and growth, whether within yourself or with your partner. Fatherhood allows us to better understand ourselves, to show greater compassion toward our partners, and to create more intentional moments with our children. It's not about having all the answers. It's about being willing to do the work, to ask questions, to listen, to learn, and to show up with purpose, even on the messy days.

That, to me, is what *Finding Fatherhood* is all about.

# Where's the Blueprint

*"No one hands you a guidebook when you become a father. You're figuring it out as you go."*

Fatherhood has a way of reshaping everything you thought you knew about life. There's no manual, no blueprint, just the unfolding of something bigger than you. It starts with a moment: hearing the news that you're going to be a dad. And from there, nothing is quite the same.

The joy is real, but so is the uncertainty. You find yourself navigating sleepless nights and quiet victories, learning to let go of perfection and embrace presence. Each milestone: first smile, first steps, the first time they really look to you for guidance, becomes a marker not just of their growth, but of yours too.

It's a journey full of contradictions: you feel stretched and grounded, exhausted yet alive. And while you can't prepare for every twist, it's in those unscripted moments that you find the heart of what it means to be a father. Not in knowing all the answers, but in choosing to grow, to show up, and to love deeply through it all.

There comes a moment when you realise that life will never be what it once was. No matter how tightly you try to hold on to the familiar rhythms, something deep has shifted. The world you knew quietly dissolves, replaced by a new reality that demands more of you than ever before.

Embracing this next chapter doesn't look the same for everyone. For some, there's a quiet sense of readiness. For others, it hits like a tidal wave. An overwhelming current of expectation and emotion. That sense of responsibility, of being someone's anchor in the world, can settle in like weight on your shoulders. And with it come the questions:

"Am I ready for this?"

"What if I mess it up?"

"What does it mean to be the kind of father my child deserves?"

These thoughts aren't signs of weakness; they're echoes of love and care. They connect you to the fathers who came before, all facing their own doubts beneath a brave face. And nestled within that uncertainty lies something quietly profound: a rare opportunity to shape a life, yes... but also to reshape your own. To build a legacy not from perfection, but from presence. To discover a love so vast and transformative that it redefines your sense of self. The kind that's not rooted in having all the answers, but in showing up anyway. That's where the real strength lives.

The role of fathers has come a long way. It wasn't that long ago that being a "good dad" mostly meant putting food on the table, providing and protecting. Often standing slightly outside the emotional world of the family. Feelings, caregiving, the tender stuff? That was seen as "mum's domain". But that old script is being rewritten.

Today, fatherhood looks and feels different. More dads are stepping fully into the day-to-day lives of their kids from packing lunchboxes, managing midnight wakeups, showing up not just physically but emotionally too. And with growing support from things like shared parental leave and more flexible work cultures, fathers are being given the space to show up in ways that were once out of reach.

It's not about replacing old roles, it's about expanding what it means to be a father. To nurture. To lead with empathy. To model vulnerability and strength at the same time. It's a shift that's changing families for the better, one moment of presence at a time.

## The changing role of Fathers

According to a 2021 Pew Research Centre study, fathers today are spending nearly three times more time with their children than dads did in the 1960s. Back then, the average was just 2.5 hours a week on childcare. Now? It's risen to more than 8 hours. And it's not just about time. A study from the National Centre for Fathering found that 72% of fathers today describe themselves as actively involved in their children's lives this is up from just 47% in the 1970s.

These aren't just statistics. They mark a quiet revolution in what fatherhood looks like. Men are stepping more fully into their role as parents, no longer defined solely by how much they provide, but by how deeply they connect. The shift isn't just changing families; it's reshaping what it means to be a man. Vulnerability, presence, empathy and growth. These aren't side notes anymore; they're central to the script we're writing as modern fathers.

This evolution calls for courage. It asks us to reflect, to adapt, to lead not with bravado but with intention. And in doing so, we get to help shape something lasting, not just in our children's lives, but in the cultural legacy of what fatherhood truly means.

Being a dad isn't a part-time gig, nor is it reserved for weekends or special occasions. It's who you are, day in and day out. And that identity doesn't live in a vacuum. It sits right alongside your career, your relationships, your personal goals, and your need for personal time. Fatherhood weaves itself into every corner of your life, often in quiet, unspoken ways.

*"You never really 'arrive' as a father. You just keep learning, adjusting, showing up."*

---

With that comes a natural tension. An ongoing dance between competing demands and limited time. You might find yourself pulled between ambition and presence, between financial pressure and bedtime stories. The responsibilities haven't shrunk; they've expanded. And with them, so can the weight of expectation. That tug-of-war can leave you stretched thin, second-guessing whether you're showing up fully in any one area.

These feelings don't mean you're failing, they mean you care. They mean you're asking the hard questions. And in that space between striving and stillness, you begin to define what balance looks like for you. Not perfect, but intentional. Not divided, but deeply integrated.

In many ways, the past decade has ushered in a quiet pressure on fathers to "do it all." To be the loving, engaged dad. The supportive, present partner. The committed professional climbing toward success. And while these roles are meaningful, the weight of balancing them can feel relentless. It pushes men to confront their limits, make hard choices, and question long-held social expectations that don't always fit the reality of modern life.

But there's a quiet upside to that tension. The act of prioritising, or put differently, choosing with intention, can lead to something far richer. A life that's more aligned. More present. One where emotional connection takes centre stage, not as an extra, but as the foundation. As fathers embrace this shift, they're creating deeper bonds with their children, nurturing relationships that are built not just on presence, but on emotional depth.

Today, we're encouraged to name what we feel, to model vulnerability, and to create space for our kids to do the same. These aren't small changes, they're generational ones. And as we help our children grow into emotionally aware, resilient human beings, we're also rewriting what strength looks like. Not in silence or sacrifice, but in openness, connection, and care.

Success isn't one-size-fits-all. It's yours to define. Maybe it shows up in the work you do, the pride you take in providing, the depth of your relationships, or the quiet contentment of an unrushed Saturday with your family. The beauty is, there's space for all of it.

More and more, fathers are finding fulfilment in places that were once overlooked or undervalued. We're beginning to write a new definition of success. One that embraces emotional presence, nurtures connection, and makes room for both ambition and tenderness. And in doing so, we're quietly challenging the outdated moulds of what it means to be a man, a provider, a father.

This isn't about grand gestures or standing on a soapbox. It's about living with intention. Showing what care looks like through your daily choices. Modelling balance, emotional integrity, and healthy relationships. That alone reshapes the narrative for your kids, your peers, and the next generation of fathers coming up behind you.

## What is *Finding Fatherhood*

*Finding Fatherhood* isn't a parenting manual. It's not a checklist for becoming a "good dad," nor is it a playbook for navigating gender politics or social commentary. That was never the intention. This book was born out of conversations. Real, open-hearted reflections shared by fathers from all walks of life. It doesn't pretend to speak for everyone, and it certainly doesn't claim to have all the answers.

What it does offer is a window into the internal world of fatherhood. The quiet doubts, the private hopes, the messy tension between who we thought we were and who we're becoming. While it's written with men in mind, it doesn't aim to reinforce old gender roles or ignore the diversity of modern families. If anything, it acknowledges its own limits. This book doesn't reflect a partner's point of view or a child's. It doesn't try to keep pace with every current cultural conversation.

Instead, it holds space for something simpler and maybe more essential: reflection, connection, and the shared humanity of fatherhood. And in doing that, maybe it helps widen the lens just a little to make room for others to do the same.

At its heart, *Finding Fatherhood* is just that, a journey written by a father, for fathers. It doesn't promise to be a guidebook or a set of instructions. Instead, it offers something more personal: a space to reflect, connect, and find reassurance in the shared stories of others navigating the early years of parenthood.

This book is an invitation. Whether you're preparing for the birth of your first child, adjusting to the chaos and wonder of a newborn, or juggling the needs of multiple young children, *Finding Fatherhood* is here for you. Not to tell you how to do it, but to walk alongside you as you figure it out. To offer insights, practical tools, and moments of reflection drawn from the lived experiences of other fathers who've faced the same questions, doubts, and joys.

There's no single "right" way to do this. Fatherhood is as varied and personal as the men who embrace it. Shaped by your values, your relationships, your circumstances, and your child's unique spirit. *Finding Fatherhood* doesn't try to define the role, it seeks to holds space for the many ways it can be lived, with courage, honesty, and love.

Whether you're stepping into fatherhood for the first time or navigating its familiar yet ever-changing terrain, it can often feel like uncharted territory.

You find yourself asking questions you never knew you'd carry:

"Am I doing this right?"

"How do I balance everything: work, family, myself?"

"Will I ever feel truly capable?"

These thoughts can feel deeply personal like you're the only one having them, but they're not. They echo across generations and across cultures. They remind us that fatherhood isn't just about raising children. It's about growing into yourself, too. It's about learning, adjusting, stumbling, and continuing to show up, day after day.

Because at its core, fatherhood is a journey of self-discovery, an invitation to become more aware, more grounded, and, ultimately, more human.

*Finding Fatherhood* was born out of conversations that were raw, unfiltered, and deeply honest exchanges with fathers from all walks of life. Entrepreneurs. Corporate leaders. Community advocates. Creatives. Each navigating the unpredictable terrain of raising young children while chasing their professional goals. Together, these voices formed a rich tapestry; woven from insights, stumbles, breakthroughs, and the quiet, universal truths of what it means to be a dad today.

At its core, this book aims to honour the threads that connect fathers everywhere: the desire to love deeply, guide thoughtfully, support intentionally, and still hold space for our own dreams. It's not about prescribing the path, it's about recognising the many ways fatherhood can be lived and expressed.

*Finding Fatherhood* is shaped to mirror the journey itself: nonlinear, evolving, and deeply personal. Some pages offer grounded tools and strategies like how to build routines, stay present amidst distraction, and carve out moments of meaning. Others dive into the emotional undercurrents: facing fears, finding your footing, and building the kind of resilience that lasts.

This is a book written in motion. Meant to walk beside you, not ahead of you.

Above all, *Finding Fatherhood* is a reminder: you are not alone. The voices in these pages come from different paths, different backgrounds, experiences, and beliefs, but their stories echo a shared truth. A thread of love, perseverance, and growth runs through them all.

---

*"I used to think joy was some big, shiny thing. Now it's a quiet Sunday morning and their head on my shoulder."*

---

Their honesty isn't just storytelling; it's an open door. An invitation to pause, reflect, and acknowledge your own journey. To honour your wins, however small they may feel. To meet your challenges not with shame, but with grace. With courage. With the quiet strength that comes from knowing you're walking this path alongside countless others.

Because fatherhood, in all its mess and beauty, is not meant to be walked alone.

## A message for Fathers

At its core, fatherhood is about showing up. Not just being there in the room but being there fully. Emotionally. Mentally. Spiritually. It's about leaning into imperfection, and recognising that the effort itself like the act of trying, of caring, of returning to your child again and again is its own kind of love.

Sometimes that love shows up in the big moments. But more often, it lives in the small ones. In the 2 a.m. feeds, the after-work playtime, the way you pause to listen when you could have rushed past. These aren't just passing gestures. They're threads that, over time, weave a childhood. A connection. A foundation.

And as time moves forward, fatherhood becomes something else, too: legacy. Every laugh, lesson, boundary, and embrace adds to the story your child will carry into the world. It's not about being perfect, it's about being present. It's about living with honesty, modelling compassion, and walking with courage through life's messiness.

That's the gift we leave behind. Not just what we taught but how we loved.

As you step into these pages, come with an open mind, an open heart, and a willingness to engage, not just with the words, but with your own story. *Finding Fatherhood* isn't here to tell you how it should be done. It's here to walk alongside you. Take what resonates, adapt what fits your world, and let the rest pass through gently. There's no single "right" way to be a father—only the path that's right for you.

The journey won't always be straight. It'll twist, stall, even overwhelm you at times. But it will also move you, shape you, and offer rewards deeper than words can hold. This book is a quiet companion on that path that acts as a reminder that even in the chaos and exhaustion, there's beauty, joy, and great responsibility to be found.

It's a celebration of those who've come before us. A tribute to the dads navigating it now, in all their complexity. And a gift to those who will one day pick up the mantle and continue to redefine what it means to be a father.

Welcome to *Finding Fatherhood*.

# Reflective Questions

Take the time to reflect on these questions:

1. What assumptions did you carry into fatherhood, and where did they come from?
2. How have your expectations about being a father changed since you began?
3. What does "doing it your way" as a father mean to you right now?

# Our Shared Experience

*"We all want our kids to feel safe, loved, and confident to be themselves."*

Across cultures, communities, and generations, certain truths seem to echo through the experience of fatherhood, creating threads that weave across continents and lifetimes. These shared understandings don't erase the individuality of each father's journey, but they offer something anchoring: the sense that we're part of something bigger. That beneath all the differences in language, tradition, and circumstance, there is a common heartbeat. A set of aspirations, values, and quiet lessons that shape the way we raise our children.

When you become a father, you often step into the role already carrying a silent blueprint. Some pieces are inherited. Drawn from your own upbringing, your relationship with your father or father-figures. Others are quietly shaped by societal cues: what you've been told, shown, or expected to believe about what a "real dad" does or doesn't do. These assumptions create a kind of internal framework, sometimes helpful, sometimes limiting, sometime unknowingly influencing how you approach this role, especially in the beginning.

But over time, fatherhood invites you to question those assumptions. To keep what aligns with your truth. To let go of what doesn't. And to build a new framework. One rooted not in expectation, but in intention.

Beyond the assumptions you may carry into fatherhood are your own aspirations. Influencing the hopes for the kind of parent, partner, and person you want to be. These aspirations come in many forms. Maybe it's wanting to be the "fun dad", the emotionally steady one, the provider who always shows up. Maybe it's about raising a brilliant mind or nurturing athletic talent. Or perhaps, more deeply, it's about breaking a cycle and choosing to create something new where there once was pain or absence.

These ambitions give direction and energy to the fatherhood journey. They help you stay anchored through late nights, big emotions, and unpredictable days. But they can also pile on pressure, especially when you're holding them quietly, or measuring yourself against them without support.

---

*"Fatherhood strips away everything that doesn't matter. What's left is love, legacy, and presence."*

---

How you carry these aspirations matters. Sharing them with your partner creates space for alignment, support, and honesty. Building a plan around them, something flexible and real, can shift them from vague expectations into meaningful intention. Because when you move from pressure to purpose, you give those aspirations a chance to become part of your parenting, not a burden on it.

While fatherhood is deeply personal, it's also part of a story that stretches back through generations. Countless men have walked this path. Each with their own hopes, doubts, and quiet moments of not knowing what comes next. Remembering that can offer much-needed perspective, especially in the moments when everything feels overwhelming or uncertain.

Recognising the universal truths that thread through fatherhood. The shared fears, the deep love, the desire to get it right, can be a steadying force. It reminds you that you're not alone. You're part of a long, imperfect, beautiful line of men doing their best. And sometimes, that reminder is enough to help you take the next step forward.

## Our assumptions

One of the most enduring assumptions around fatherhood is the idea that a father's primary role is to provide. For generations, cultural norms have cast fathers as the breadwinners, the ones who ensure financial security while leaving caregiving and emotional labour to someone else. And while the need to provide materially still matters, the landscape has changed.

Today, being a father means more than bringing home a paycheque. There's a growing expectation to show up emotionally, to nurture, to comfort, to be present not just in body, but in heart and mind. Workplace reforms, evolving partnerships, and the rising aspirations of both parents have helped expand what fatherhood can look like. But with that shift comes new pressure. We're still unlearning the message that a man's worth is measured by his income, even as we try to offer bedtime stories and carry the invisible weight of emotional care.

Balancing these roles is no small task. The tug between providing and being present, between tradition and transformation, can feel relentless. But naming that pressure, by acknowledging its weight we're taking the first step in loosening its grip. Because your value as a father isn't found in one narrow role. It lives in the choices you make each day to show up, fully, in a way that's true to you.

One of the most persistent assumptions many fathers carry into parenthood is the belief that they're supposed to have all the answers. That they need to be the unwavering source of wisdom, the strong and steady one, always ready with the right response or solution. But here's the truth: no one has all the answers. And believing you should can set an impossible standard.

Parenting isn't a test you pass. It's a journey you grow through. It's full of unknowns, curveballs, and countless moments where you feel unsure. And yet, it's in those messy, uncharted spaces that some of the most meaningful growth happens, not just for your child, but for you. Mistakes, far from being signs of failure, become some of the most powerful learning tools you'll have.

Then there's the other common myth: that fatherhood will come naturally. That instinct alone will guide you through. While there may be moments of deep intuition, the truth is that much of parenting is learned through repetition, patience, and resilience. You try, you stumble, you adapt. And then you try again.

Waiting to feel "fully ready" can create pressure that sets you up for quiet disappointment. When things don't come easily, when you're exhausted, frustrated, or feeling like you're not enough, it's easy to assume you're falling short. But in reality, you're doing the work. You're in it. And that effort, that devotion, is what matters most

Amid all the assumptions and expectations, these can be both spoken and unspoken, there are also your aspirations. The dreams you carry not just for your child, but for the kind of father you want to be. The kind of partner, guide, protector, and presence you hope to embody.

These aspirations can be quiet or bold, detailed or just a feeling. You might envision raising a child who's kind, confident, curious about the world. Or you might be striving to be the dad who's steady when things get messy. The partner who holds space, listens deeply, and grows alongside the family you're building. These hopes aren't separate from the challenges, they live right alongside them, fuelling your intentions even when the road gets uncertain.

What matters isn't whether you achieve every one of them, it's that you care enough to hold them. That you're willing to reflect, adjust, and keep showing up in service of them. These aspirations are not a burden. They are a compass. They point you toward the kind of fatherhood that's most meaningful to you.

## Our aspirations

One of the most common aspirations we bring into fatherhood is the hope that our children will grow up happy, confident, and kind. It's a dream rooted not just in what we want for them, but in who we're trying to be ourselves. We want to give them tools, not just to succeed, but to thrive. To meet life with resilience. To respond to others with empathy. To face challenges with quiet courage.

These values don't appear overnight. They're passed on in subtle, everyday moments from how we speak, how we show patience when it's hard, how we keep showing up even when we're tired. Modelling kindness, emotional honesty, and perseverance doesn't just teach these traits. It weaves them into the fabric of your home, creating a space where those values aren't just taught, they're lived.

And when hard times come, as they inevitably do, it's those very values that help keep the household steady. Not because things are always perfect, but because the ground beneath has been shaped by love, consistency, and intention.

*"It doesn't matter where you're from—every father I know worries he's not doing enough."*

Another meaningful aspiration many fathers carry is the desire to build a strong, trusting, and respectful relationship with their child, one that goes beyond simply being an authority figure. You may hope to be a confidant, a mentor, a coach, even a friend. This kind of bond doesn't happen by accident. It requires consistent, intentional effort. It's built in the everyday choices to listen, to speak with honesty, to create a space where your child feels safe being fully themselves.

Over time, that foundation of trust becomes the thread that holds your relationship together, even as your child grows and changes.

For many of us, these aspirations are shaped by our own histories. Everyone's upbringing is different and, in some cases, the father you hope to be may stand in direct contrast to the one you had. Maybe you're aiming to break a generational pattern, to rewrite a story that didn't serve you. Or maybe you're drawing on the strength of what you were given, hoping to carry those values forward with intention.

Becoming a father offers a rare opportunity to pause and reflect. To look honestly at what shaped you, and to decide, deliberately, what you want to carry forward and what you're ready to leave behind. It's in this reflection that the heart of intentional parenting lives.

In time, you may come to realise that some things need to be done differently. That being emotionally present matters just as much (if not more) than being efficient or prepared. That nurturing your child's individuality, supporting their dreams, and creating a home where they can feel seen and safe is its own powerful legacy.

How you choose to show up in your child's life becomes an act of intention. A compass that helps guide your decisions, even when the road feels messy or uncertain. And from that place of intention, a deeper sense of purpose can begin to take root.

Because beyond hopes and goals, fatherhood often becomes a calling. A quiet, everyday way of contributing to a better future. That sense of purpose transcends background, culture, or circumstance. It reminds us that while every father's story is unique, the heart of fatherhood: presence, care, and connection, is something we all share.

## Our desires

One of the most fundamental desires many fathers carry, often quietly is the need to feel valued. To be recognised not just for the big moments, but for the countless small, invisible acts that keep a family running. Whether it's finding the lost toy, repairing the wobbly table leg, or simply being the steady presence in the room, fathers want to know their contributions matter. That their effort has weight. That they're seen.

And it goes both ways. Just as we yearn to be appreciated, so too does our partner. A kind word, a long hug, a message sent in the middle of a busy day, simple small gestures like these help reinforce the shared foundation you're building together. They remind each other that you're in this side-by-side.

And then there's something else. Something you may not fully expect: the deep desire to protect. To create safety and security for your child and your partner. You may understand this conceptually, but when it lands in your body, when you feel it as instinct, as purpose; it changes you. That sense of responsibility becomes more than a role. It becomes part of who you are.

It's natural to want to shield your child from harm, both physical and emotional. That protective instinct is powerful and deeply rooted in love. It shows up in countless small ways: childproofing the home, setting boundaries at the playground, offering guidance on friendships, and stepping in when trouble feels close. It's a quiet promise we make to our children, that we are here to keep them safe.

But with that promise comes a delicate balance. Because growth, by its very nature, requires vulnerability. Scraped knees, hurt feelings, hard lessons, they're all part of becoming resilient, empathetic, and emotionally aware. And sometimes, in our effort to protect, we can unintentionally step in too soon, shielding our children from experiences that could help them grow.

The challenge is not in silencing that instinct; it's in refining it. Learning when to hold close, and when to let go. Trusting that your presence, your guidance, and your love will give your child the foundation they need to navigate life's inevitable challenges. Not immune to them but equipped for them.

Perhaps the deepest and most enduring desire you'll carry as a father is the longing to share moments of joy and connection with your child. Amid the noise and pace of daily life, it's often the simple, unstructured moments that stay with you. The laughter over a silly game, the quiet storytelling before bed, or the spontaneous dance in the kitchen. These moments, seemingly small, hold immense weight. They remind you of the pure, unfiltered love that defines your bond.

They also ground you. When the days are long, patience is thin, or life feels overwhelming, these memories become a quiet refuge, a reminder that at the core of all the challenges is love. That your child, in their own way, is always reaching for you. Wanting your time. Craving your presence. And those moments of shared joy don't just matter, they become the foundation of your relationship.

## Lessons

One of the most profound aspects of fatherhood is the ongoing personal growth it demands, and the transformation it quietly creates. As you move through this journey, you'll face moments that stretch you, reshape your views, and reorient your priorities. Often, it's not the big milestones that teach you the most, but the small, quiet lessons that come when you least expect them.

Patience is one of the earliest (and hardest) of those lessons. In the newborn phase, when so much of your child's care is centred on their mother, you might find yourself unsure where you fit. You'll wonder how to help, what your partner needs, what your baby needs, or even what value you bring.

But here's where patience and presence become intertwined. Sometimes, the most meaningful act is simply showing up. Being in the room. Creating calm when everything feels chaotic. Not rushing to fix things, but offering your presence as a steadying force.

It can feel uncomfortable, even disorienting, especially if you're used to solving problems or being "useful" in a tangible way. But one of the most humbling truths of early fatherhood is this: your presence can be enough. Your partner doesn't always need solutions. Your child doesn't need perfection. What they need is you, choosing to stay, to notice, to quietly support, even when you're not the centre of the moment.

This isn't about being passive. It's about being attuned. It's about learning that sometimes love looks like holding space, not fixing, not leading, just being there. And that's one of the strongest things you can offer.

The old analogy that life is a marathon, not a sprint, rings especially true in parenting. Raising children is, at its core, an act of endurance. A long journey shaped by persistence, patience, and the quiet strength to keep showing up. It's working through sleepless nights, navigating tantrums, soothing bumped heads and scraped knees, and handling emotional storms with as much calm as you can muster.

Patience isn't just helpful: it's essential. And it's a lesson you'll relearn, again and again. Parenting asks you to meet defiance with composure, chaos with steadiness. It also asks something quietly courageous: to confront your own emotional triggers. To recognise the moments when your first reaction may not serve the moment. To pause, reflect, and try again. You won't get it right every time. That's not failure. It's fatherhood.

And then there's the lesson every dad learns early, often without words: your child doesn't want the biggest toy or the most perfect day. What they want more than anything is you. Not just there, but present. Not distracted. Not half-listening. Just fully with them in the small, ordinary moments that build an extraordinary bond.

Presence isn't measured in minutes; it's measured in attention. In the eye contact during story time. In the undivided laughter during a shared joke. In the stillness when they need comfort. These are the quiet beats of parenting that ask us to reevaluate what really matters and to find space for what does

Fatherhood, more than almost anything else, teaches humility. Children have a way of revealing your limitations, not out of malice, but through their raw need, their questions, their mirror-like honesty. You're reminded, often abruptly, that you don't have all the answers. That you'll make mistakes. That you'll lose patience, misread cues, say the wrong thing. And yet, in those moments, there's something beautiful: the realisation that you're still learning. Still growing. Still becoming.

Humility, in that sense, is a gift. It invites grace toward your child, your partner, and most importantly, yourself. It reminds you that growth doesn't stop when you become a parent; it begins again, in new and unexpected ways. And when the day has stretched you thin, that humble mindset becomes a comfort: tomorrow is another day. No matter how hard today was or how beautiful, "this too shall pass". That mantra softens the edges. It helps you ride the waves, moment to moment, with just a little more steadiness.

But perhaps the most transformative lesson of all is love. The kind of love that arrives the moment your child enters the world and never leaves. It doesn't depend on milestones. It doesn't disappear in frustration. It's unconditional. It wraps around you in the quietest, most surprising ways. In a sleepy cuddle, a spontaneous giggle, and the gentle weight of their trust.

This love becomes your anchor. Your reason to keep going when the path ahead feels blurry. It doesn't demand perfection. It simply calls you to keep showing up with softness, with presence, with whatever you have to give. And in return, it offers something rare: a quiet clarity. A feeling in your chest that reminds you you're exactly where you need to be, even when it's messy, and even when it's hard.

Children look to their fathers for connection, guidance, and support, and the love they offer in return is unfiltered and full. Few things compare to the feeling of a child running into your arms at the end of a long day, or the spark of joy in their eyes when you enter the room each morning. These moments remind us that, no matter what the outside world holds, we are their safe place.

*"No matter where you come from, every father I've met just wants to be better than the one before him."*

As you walk this path, you'll find fatherhood is filled with joy, growth, and moments of self-discovery that leave lasting imprints on your heart. Yes, the journey is marked by challenges, but the role of a father, and a partner, is also one of life's richest, most rewarding experiences.

The wonder of being a father goes far beyond the surface. It lives in the deep emotional connections you build, in the quiet lessons you learn, and in the simple, extraordinary privilege of watching your child grow into themselves—with your steady presence close behind.

While the truths of fatherhood, its assumptions, aspirations, desires, and hard-won lessons, may feel universal, they are also deeply personal. No two journeys are the same. Your path is shaped by your values, your experiences, and the ever-evolving landscape of your own life. What speaks to one father may not resonate with another, and that's not just okay, it's the beauty of it.

Fatherhood isn't meant to be uniform. It's meant to be lived. And the richness of that experience lies in its diversity, in the countless ways men show up for their children, their partners, and themselves.

The invitation is simply this: approach it all with openness and curiosity. Be willing to learn. To grow. To listen, both to others and to yourself. Take what feels true from the stories around you, seek wisdom from those who walk ahead, and stay rooted in your own unfolding truth.

Because fatherhood, at its best, isn't about perfection. It's about presence. And the courage to keep becoming.

# Reflective Questions

Take the time to reflect on these questions:

1. What assumptions about fatherhood did you inherit—from culture, family, or society, and which ones have you had to challenge or redefine?
2. What do you think your children would say about you as their father?
3. What are the fears you carry silently, and how are they impacting you and your approach to parenting?

# The Starting Point

*"You've got to start with trust. If they trust you, they'll come to you when it matters."*

While your journey through fatherhood will be uniquely your own, you're not walking it alone. The fears you carry, the hopes you hold, the aspirations you nurture, and the challenges you meet, these are felt by parents across every walk of life. They ebb and flow through different stages, rising with intensity in some seasons, softening in others.

Reflecting on these highs and lows reminds us of a vital truth: fatherhood was never meant to be perfect. It was meant to grow us. To teach us. To stretch us in the direction of love and courage. It's about showing up, day-after-day with patience and presence, when it's hard, when you're tired, and with love, which doesn't always need to be loud to be deeply felt.

It's about embracing the mess, welcoming the emotion, and leaning into the beautifully imperfect rhythm of raising a child. And in that rhythm, amid the struggle, the laughter, and the quiet victories; you'll find joy. A joy that changes you. A joy that lingers

As you continue to walk your own path as a father, let these truths be your compass. Know that you're not alone in your struggles or your victories. Across the globe, fathers are waking up each day with the same hopes, the same doubts, the same quiet desire to do right by their children.

Fatherhood offers something rare in this world: the chance to leave a legacy built not on perfection, but on presence. To shape the next generation through love, patience, and example. To grow into the best version of yourself, not in spite of parenting, but through it.

So, lean into it. Embrace the mess, the joy, the hard days, and the heart-expanding ones. Because the truth is, the rewards of fatherhood, those small, extraordinary moments of connection will always outweigh the challenges. And in the end, they're what last.

There is no single blueprint for fatherhood. No universal map. Each father's approach is shaped by a unique blend of social norms, cultural influences, life experience, economic realities, and personal temperament. And yet, in the absence of a clear standard, many of us find ourselves looking sideways, measuring ourselves against other fathers, or even against the memory of our own.

---

*"I feared my past would become their foundation—and I didn't want that."*

---

We compare how often we're home, how patient we are at bedtime, how confidently our children navigate the world. We notice which kids are hitting milestones first, which ones sleep through the night, which seem more outgoing, curious, or emotionally tuned in. Often, this isn't born of judgment; it's instinctive. A quiet search for reassurance that we're "on track."

But comparison, while human, can pull us away from what matters most: connection. That's why it's so important to return to foundational truths. To remember that fatherhood is not a competition, but a commitment. Not a performance, but a practice. It's about presence, adaptability, and love, not perfection or keeping pace.

The point is not to eliminate comparison. It's to recognise it, then recenter. To reflect on what matters most to you and your family. And to build your own definition of fatherhood grounded in intention, not assumption.

## Every child is unique

Every child arrives with their own personality, needs, and way of engaging with the world. What works effortlessly for one child might completely miss the mark with another, even within the same family. That's the paradox and the gift of parenting: there is no single formula.

You'll find yourself adjusting; sometimes slowly, sometimes in the moment, your own approach to suit each child's temperament, interests, and stage of development. Strategies you once trusted may suddenly falter. What brought connection yesterday may bring frustration today. And that's not a sign you're doing something wrong. It's a sign you're paying attention.

The key is flexibility. A willingness to reflect, to talk openly with your partner, and to revisit what's working and what isn't. Parenting is dynamic. And sometimes, success is simply about finding what works for now, 9for this phase, this emotion, this challenge. Then, trying again tomorrow with fresh eyes.

## Family structures vary

Families take many forms. Some are traditional, others are single-parent households, blended families, same-sex parent families, or something entirely unique. Each structure brings its own dynamics, its own patterns of connection, challenge, and strength, that shape how parenting is experienced.

But beyond these differences, the heartbeat of a family is universal. Love that endures. Communication that builds trust. Forgiveness when things unravel. And a shared willingness to keep learning and growing together.

What defines a strong family isn't its structure. It's the intention behind how they show up for each other.

## Cultural expectation differ

Cultural norms and traditions play a powerful role in shaping how we understand and express parenthood. In some cultures, a father might be expected to lead with authority and discipline; in others, he might be encouraged to prioritise nurturing and emotional connection. These inherited roles carry weight. They're woven into family expectations, community narratives, and even your own internal voice.

But fatherhood also invites a quiet reckoning. A moment to pause and ask: What kind of father do I want to be? Sometimes, that means leaning into the values you've been given. Other times, it means respectfully questioning them. You may find yourself balancing the respect you have for cultural expectations with a desire to parent differently, enabling you to be more emotionally available or more attuned.

Carving out your own identity as a father isn't always easy. It can bring discomfort, especially when your choices differ from those around you. But there's strength in that discomfort, it's a reminder that you're parenting with intention. That you're choosing love over habit. Presence over prescription.

At the heart of it, fatherhood is a conversation between where you come from and where you want to go. And in that space, even the smallest acts of conscious parenting can become acts of quiet transformation.

## Society is evolving

As societal norms around masculinity, gender roles, and work-life balance continue to evolve, so too does the experience of fatherhood. Today, fathers are navigating expectations that extend far beyond traditional roles. We're expected not only to provide but to be present. To chase ambition without sacrificing connection. To succeed at work while showing up wholeheartedly at home.

This is a shift that many in previous generations may not have had to contend with so fully. There is no roadmap for how to balance these dual roles. No single script to follow. And yet, in that absence lies an invitation.

The lack of a blueprint creates space for something powerful: the chance to redefine what fatherhood can look like for you. To write a new story about success, one that includes professional ambition and bedtime stories. Strategic thinking and giggling moments on the living room floor. It won't be easy. The push and pull can be real and relentless. But it's not a path you need to walk alone, and it's not one without its rewards.

In redefining fatherhood, you're not only shaping your child's world, you're also reclaiming your own. One choice, one boundary, one meaningful moment at a time.

## Watching your child discover the world

Children see the world with eyes unclouded by routine, and as a father, you're invited to see it alongside them. Their joy at the crunch of autumn leaves, their surprised squint at the tartness of a lemon, or the spellbound way they watch ants marching across a footpath. These small moments hold profound magic. Through them, you're reminded to slow down. To notice. To rediscover the beauty in life's simplest pleasures.

Even familiar places like a walk through the same park trail, the same corner café, the same patch of grass suddenly feel new when experienced through your child's wonder. Every puddle becomes an ocean. Every stick, a sword. Their world is wide open, and in walking beside them, yours expands too.

Of course, these adventures often come with detours. Slowed pace for tired legs. Repeated questions. Pauses for tears or treasure hunts. They're delightful and occasionally exasperating. But in these pauses lives one of parenthood's greatest teachers: patience.

## Rediscover joy through their eyes

Raising a child has a remarkable way of slowing you down and inviting you to notice what you might otherwise rush past. The small things: the shape of a cloud, the crunch of a sandy trail underfoot, the playful possibilities of a cardboard box. Through your child's eyes, the world becomes textured again. full of magic, mystery, and surprise.

---

*"Before I could give my kids stability, I had to find it in myself."*

---

This sense of wonder often emerges in the most ordinary places. These shared moments aren't just fun, they're grounding. They remind you what it feels like to be fully present. To play. To see the world not through the lens of a schedule, but through curiosity and connection.

In many ways, your child becomes your teacher guiding you back to joy, reminding you how rich life can be when you simply slow down enough to notice it.

## Becoming a teacher and learning

Fatherhood is as much a process of learning as it is of teaching. Yes, fathers often step into the role of teacher offering guidance, sharing skills, and passing down hard-earned wisdom. Whether it's helping a child learn to kick a ball, write their name, whistle for the first time, or navigate the delicate landscape of friendship, these moments offer more than just instruction, they create connection.

But with each lesson given, there's one being received. Your child teaches you as well. Often about patience, perspective, resilience, and joy. You may show them how to tie their shoes, but they'll show you how to find meaning in the mundane. You may help them through their first clash on the playground, but they'll teach you what it means to love without conditions.

Whether building something side-by-side, problem-solving in the aisle of a supermarket, or working through a tough emotional moment, fathers and children grow together. It's in these small, often overlooked moments that lasting bonds are built and character is quietly shaped, for both of you.

At the same time, you're constantly learning from your child. Their perspective is unfiltered, curious, and often unexpectedly wise has a way of reframing the familiar. They ask questions that make you pause, offer observations that make you laugh, and extend love in ways that catch you off guard. In these moments, you're reminded not just of who they are becoming, but of who you are becoming.

Children have a quiet power to inspire change, not through pressure, but through presence. They invite you to slow down, to speak more kindly, to stretch beyond your limits. They challenge your assumptions and reveal your blind spots. And in doing so, they nudge you toward becoming a better version of yourself, not just as a father, but as a person.

## Celebrating everyday moments

While growth milestones and developmental achievements hold their place, the true beauty of fatherhood often lives in the everyday. In the warmth of morning cuddles, the chorus of laughter over dinner, the quiet reassurance of a bedtime chat—these small, seemingly ordinary moments weave together into something deeply lasting. They become the soft edges and golden threads of your child's memories.

These are the moments your child is likely to carry forward. The rituals and rhythms that offer comfort, stability, and connection. Whether it's Saturday morning pancakes, walks to the café for cake and conversation, cheering together during a game, or playing cards around the dining table, these traditions ground your relationship in joy. They tell your child: you are loved, and I'm here.

And that's the legacy. Not the perfection of parenting, but the repetition of presence. The intentional carving out of time in a busy world to build something quiet, enduring, and real.

## The magic of play

Play is one of the most powerful tools fathers have for connection. Both structured and unstructured play open up endless opportunities, not just for development, but for bonding, laughter, and shared joy. Whether you're building a pillow fort, kicking a ball around the backyard, stacking blocks, role-playing as superheroes, or sipping invisible tea from plastic cups, each playful moment creates a thread in the tapestry of your relationship.

Play is also where your child's personality begins to shine; unfiltered and alive. It's where imagination takes flight and self-expression unfolds. You'll find yourself beaming with pride the day your child builds an entire imaginary world and proudly invites you inside. There's no agenda, no right way. Just presence, wonder, and the willingness to step into their world on their terms.

These small adventures may seem fleeting, but they leave a lasting imprint. They teach your child that you're not just watching, you're with them. And in that shared space, trust deepens, and love grows.

## Leaving a lasting impact

The lessons and memories you create with your child don't just shape the present, they echo across time. Fatherhood often awakens a deeper sense of purpose, rooted in the kind of world you want to create for your child. That purpose becomes a guiding force, shaping how you show up, what you prioritise, and how intentionally you pass on the values and traditions that will inform your child's choices for years to come.

*"Our family rhythm became our foundation. Dinner, bath, bed—it sounds simple, but it holds us together."*

By modelling qualities like honesty, respect, and empathy, not just in big teachable moments, but in everyday interactions, you begin to build something that extends beyond yourself. You create a generational ripple effect. Your words, your actions, your consistency these all become part of the foundation that your child stands on as they learn to move through the world with confidence, independence, and resilience.

There is a deep pride that comes with watching your child thrive, because of the lessons they've learnt along the way from you and others. And that modelling starts long before they fully understand the words you speak. It begins in the early years, in the small gestures, the tone of your voice, the way you treat others and even how you treat yourself.

# Reflective Questions

Take the time to reflect on these questions:

1. What values are most important to you in building your family's foundation?
2. Currently what makes you feel most grounded as a father?
3. What habits or routines could help bring more stability to your family life?

# The Balancing Act

*"Some days I feel like I'm failing at both – work and home. But I keep showing up."*

One of the most significant and rarely discussed adjustments new fathers face is learning to balance the demands of work and family. While much is said about preparing for parenthood, few truly prepare you for the complexities of juggling a career, nurturing a partnership, and showing up consistently as a father.

Many fathers find themselves caught in an emotional crosscurrent, pulled between the responsibility of providing and the longing to be present. The desire to support your partner, to witness your child's milestones, to simply be there, often clashes with professional pressures and ingrained ideas of success.

This balancing act can quietly strain even the strongest relationships. Tension builds when time feels scarce, when conversations become transactional, or when emotional presence becomes harder to access after long days of work. And where there's tension, guilt often follows, especially during challenging seasons at home or in especially demanding roles.

These feelings aren't signs of weakness. They're signals. Indicators of how deeply you care and how intently you're trying to stretch across two vital parts of your life. And within that stretch lies an opportunity. Not to do everything perfectly, but to redefine what balance means for your family, your values, and the kind of father you want to become.

Post-COVID, hybrid work models have reshaped what's possible for many families. With new flexibility, some parents have been able to spend more time at home and take on caregiving roles more actively than before. In the best scenarios, workdays are designed around a child's rhythm: morning drop-offs, afternoon pick-ups, bath time, dinner, bedtime stories. It's not without effort. Flexible workplaces, clear boundaries, and thoughtful planning are often required but when it works, it creates meaningful connection and shared presence.

Of course, even with the best intentions, there will be times when work creeps in, calls that run late, emails that can't wait, and stress that spills into the living room. In those moments, it's important to zoom out. Parenting is a long game. It's not measured in perfect attendance, but in consistency, intention, and love.

*"The guilt hits you either way—if you work late, you feel it. If you leave early, you feel it."*

Your child doesn't keep score. They hold onto patterns, feelings, and how they felt in your presence over time. And what might feel like a temporary compromise like a missed bedtime or a moment of distraction, could in hindsight be the very thing that allowed you to support your family, or show up in a more grounded way tomorrow. It's not always easy, and it can feel counterintuitive but trust that what you're building is cumulative.

The overall impression you leave of being there, of showing up with care, of trying is what matters more than any one moment ever could.

## Redefining success

One of the first and most important steps in finding balance across professional and parental roles is redefining success. For many fathers, this means shifting from traditional metrics like promotions, salary increases, or accolades, to a more holistic view that also embraces personal fulfilment, emotional presence, and family wellbeing.

This isn't about diminishing the importance of career achievement or identity. For many men, ambition is not driven by gender expectations, it's born from a love of the work itself. The desire to contribute. To lead. To collaborate. To get better. That passion for work, the satisfaction of doing a job well, or the energising dynamic of being part of a team. Those things matter deeply.

But if you're holding this book in your hands, chances are you're also asking a deeper question: "How can I be ambitious in my career while still being present and engaged as a father?" You're not alone in that. And you're not wrong to want both.

Redefining success doesn't mean choosing one path over the other. It means crafting a definition that fits your values. One that accounts for who you want to be in the boardroom and in the backyard. It's about weaving your sense of purpose through all the roles you hold so that your version of success includes not just what you accomplish, but who you get to share it with.

Redefining success means recognising that being an engaged and present father is no longer a secondary aim, it's a core priority. For many of us, success was once shaped by unspoken norms: climbing the career ladder quickly, earning the title, being the "breadwinner." But something shifts, often around the time you're preparing to welcome your first child. A quiet, persistent question begins to rise: "What's the point of all this if I'm missing my kids' childhood?"

That question can be a wake-up call. It invites you to reimagine success not as a race to the top, but as a search for balance. A life where professional fulfilment and family connection are not competing forces, but coexisting values.

This shift often requires confronting long-held beliefs about work, worth, and masculinity. It means acknowledging that time spent with family isn't a distraction from your goals, it is part of what makes the pursuit of those goals meaningful in the first place.

When fathers give themselves permission to value both ambition and presence, they begin to craft a vision of success that's not only more sustainable but more deeply satisfying.

---

*"I constantly feel like I'm robbing time from one side of my life to feed the other."*

---

It can feel brutal to admit but sometimes, being present with your child may register, even briefly, as a distraction from other pressing obligations. This isn't about a lack of love or willingness. It's about the mental trade-offs we constantly make when juggling competing priorities. In those moments, we unconsciously run an equation: "Where is my focus most urgently needed?" or "What will this cost me later?" It's the classic 'sunk cost' dilemma. The tension of wanting to give your best to multiple things, knowing that something will inevitably take the back seat.

Take bedtime, for example. Your child isn't tired. They're resisting sleep. You've got a burning email to send, or a breakfast meeting on your calendar. In that moment, presence might feel less rewarding or even less "productive." But that's only true if we're measuring the moment by the wrong system.

Redefining success isn't really about success at all. It's about values. About reshuffling your internal ledger to reflect what truly matters, not just to others, but to you. It's not a rejection of ambition or achievement. It's an honest, intentional adjustment. A different way of valuing your time, your energy, and the legacy you're shaping day by day.

## The dual pull

At the heart of the parenting experience lies a persistent tension: the dual pull between work and family. On one side, careers demand time, focus, and energy with unspoken expectations around productivity, innovation, and visible outcomes. On the other, family life asks for something quieter but no less vital: emotional availability, presence, and hands-on participation in raising children and maintaining a functional, nurturing home.

These roles aren't inherently at odds but they often feel mutually exclusive. And when the demands pile up, many fathers find themselves living in a quiet undertow of guilt; questioning whether they're giving enough, achieving enough, or being present enough. It can be overwhelming to realise how often one part of your life feels like it's pulling you away from another you deeply care about.

The early days of fatherhood bring this into sharp focus. People will tell you, sometimes with a smile or sometimes as a warning, that your world will be turned upside down. And even when you understand this intellectually, the practical experience is something else entirely. It's visceral. Sleep-deprived. Chaotic. At times, disorienting. And yet, within that upheaval, a quieter truth begins to emerge: your priorities are shifting. Your sense of self is stretching. And you're learning to recalibrate not because you have to but because you want to.

It happens almost without warning. You go from working late into the night, even on weekends, to the sudden realisation that your time is no longer solely your own. You may deeply want to be present for every milestone, every bedtime story, every scraped knee. And yet, your work or perhaps your own business is hitting a critical growth point, pulling at you with urgency and purpose.

In these moments, it's easy to feel like you're being stretched across two lives that matter to you equally. And you're not alone in that.

This is a struggle shared by countless fathers, caught between the drive to excel professionally and the longing to show up meaningfully at home. The tension is made heavier by societal norms that often equate success with long hours, relentless ambition, and a constant state of productivity. Within that equation, fatherhood can feel like an add-on, when in reality, it's a role that demands (and deserves) its own kind of excellence.

Then, layered into it all, is the pressure to provide financially. To hold up the household in practical ways, even as you're trying to nurture it emotionally. It's a lot. And yet, acknowledging this tension is not a sign of failure, it's a sign of presence. Of caring. Of trying, each day, to build a life that reflects all that you value

## Strategies for balance

There's no one-size-fits-all answer to the balance between career and fatherhood. The path is often carved out of necessity to avoid burnout, protect your health, or preserve your relationships. For some, it's about ensuring you're contributing equally to the mental and emotional load at home. For others, it's the simple, joyful desire to soak up more of this fleeting time with your child.

Regardless of the motivation, fathers across the world are reshaping the way they work and parent. They're experimenting with strategies, trying workarounds, and forging new routines that make space for both ambition and connection. These approaches aren't always perfect, but they're real, lived, and hard-won.

What they tend to have in common is this: intentional planning, honest communication, and a willingness to adapt. To say, "this isn't working" and try again. To name what matters and make space for it. To honour your family without abandoning your professional self.

## Dedicated planning

For dual-income households where both parents work or carry major commitments, balancing the demands of work and family life often calls for creativity, communication, and shared effort. Daily responsibilities don't wait. Appointments need booking, meals need preparing, washing piles up, and downtime remains essential.

Many families find ways to coordinate schedules so that at least one parent is available during key transitions like school pickups, drop-offs, or doctor's appointments. For others, the glue is visibility. Whether it's a shared digital calendar or a magnetic weekly planner stuck on the fridge, knowing each other's commitments creates a sense of rhythm and trust.

Equally important is carving out time to check in with your partner for weekly chats to review what's coming up, align on logistics, and flag any high-stress moments before they hit. These rituals don't just prevent missed kid pickups, they create emotional predictability and ease some of the mental load.

In this dance, three qualities prove invaluable: communication, flexibility, and adaptability. But perhaps most essential is grace, especially in the moments where something inevitably slips. Forgiveness. A willingness to remember that you're both doing your best, and that partnership is not about perfection, but persistence.

## Time blocking

Time blocking has become a valuable strategy for fathers navigating the complex demands of work, life, and family. By assigning specific blocks of time to different responsibilities whether work, caregiving, or personal recharge, fathers can create stronger boundaries that support deeper presence and focus across all areas of life.

Establishing habits and discipline around time blocking helps clarify what's non-negotiable (like school pickups or bedtime routines), what's flexible, and where unstructured time can create breathing room. Importantly, these blocks extend beyond the typical work meetings or logistical tasks. They intentionally include things like family dinnertime, playdates, and even moments of quiet connection, ensuring those experiences are not lost in the noise of the day.

For time-poor fathers, this practice can provide a sense of clarity and control. It also signals to both colleagues and family members that time spent at home is just as meaningful and worthy of protection as time spent at work. By treating family moments as sacred appointments, not optional extras, fathers model a culture of respect, commitment, and balance.

Critics may view time blocking as rigid or overly controlled. Some may see partitioning time as selfish. But in practice, it can be the opposite: a tool for intentional living. One that frees your attention, clarifies your priorities, and bridges the gap between distraction and presence.

## Shared responsibilities

While it's often said that it takes a village to raise a child, the reality is that many families today are raising children without the support of a ready-made village of extended family and close friends. In the absence of that wider circle, balance often comes from teamwork, a partnership built on mutual trust, shared responsibility, and ongoing communication.

Fathers who embrace this collaborative model, who actively sharing parenting responsibilities, household tasks, and emotional labour, are often better equipped to navigate the dual demands of work and family life. Whether it's tag-teaming bedtime routines or championing each other's careers, this shared approach doesn't just lighten the load; it strengthens the foundation of the family itself.

If you and your partner are committed to showing up as equals, that partnership deserves intentional care. Weekly check-ins to coordinate logistics are crucial, yes—but so too are the deeper conversations. Making time to align on personal aspirations, family goals, and how you're both really doing helps ensure that your connection doesn't get lost beneath the endless to-do list.

In doing so, you're not only creating a more sustainable life—you're modelling cooperation, empathy, and mutual respect for your child. You're showing them, in real time, what a healthy, supportive partnership looks like. And that might be one of the most lasting gifts you give them.

## Setting boundaries

In today's hyper-connected world, the boundary between work and home life is increasingly porous. The buzz of an incoming email or the ping of a message can instantly fracture your focus, pulling attention away from the people right in front of you. That's why setting clear boundaries around technology and availability has become essential for fathers who want to be truly present at home.

Simple strategies like turning off work notifications during family time or designating specific hours as "no work zones" can go a long way toward protecting your energy and anchoring you in the moment. Used alongside time blocking, even small shifts like creating a 'no phone zone' at the dinner table or during bedtime can help carve out meaningful space for connection.

*"There's chaos, sure. But there's also laughter, dancing in the kitchen, and bedtime hugs."*

These boundaries are more than just rules. They're signals. They tell your partner, your children and even yourself that this time matters. That you're not just nearby, but with them.

It can feel awkward at first, especially if your work culture prizes constant accessibility. But naming and communicating your boundaries, whether it's to your boss, your team, or your family it helps to create clarity and ease. Over time, these small acts of intentionality can reshape the rhythm of your day and transform moments that might otherwise be lost to distraction into rituals of presence.

## Embrace flexibility

It's easy to assume that time blocking and boundary-setting create a rigid, almost robotic approach to daily life, especially during a season as unpredictable as early fatherhood. But in reality, these strategies offer something else entirely: a scaffold. A gentle structure to help bring clarity to a time when everything feels in flux.

That said, the need to embrace flexibility cannot be overstated. Life rarely moves in a straight line. Disruptions will happen, your child might spike a fever, a last-minute work crisis may arise, unexpected guests turn up, or a job you counted on suddenly disappears. These moments test not just your time management, but your mindset.

Flexibility is the antidote to rigidity, but it's also a form of power. For some fathers, it means rethinking what "normal" looks like: embracing night shifts, remote work, compressed weeks, or unconventional schedules to stay present at home while still fulfilling professional goals. These paths often require creativity, communication, and courage, but they can lead to a deeper, more sustainable sense of balance.

In some cases, it might even mean reimagining your career path altogether, or initiating bold conversations about what you need from your work environment to show up fully for your family. When you approach life with flexibility, you're not just reacting to change, you're redefining what success and presence look like on your own terms.

And that's the quiet gift of flexibility: it puts you back in the driver's seat. You get to choose what matters most and how you'll make space for it.

## Navigating challenges

Despite your best efforts, challenges will come. For fathers managing high-demand careers, there will be seasons of stress, moments of burnout, and quiet pangs of guilt, fuelled by feelings of falling short at work, at home, or both. You may find yourself in a swirl of internal debate, wrestling with the question: "Why am I failing at everything?"

*"I used to think balance was a destination. Now I know it's a decision I make daily."*

---

This is more common than we admit. It's a quiet truth of modern fatherhood often felt, but rarely voiced. That's why it's so important to name it. Share these feelings with your partner or a trusted friend, ideally another father who understands the terrain. In periods of stress, our self-perception becomes cloudy. By opening up, you give someone the chance to reflect back what's actually happening: what you're managing, where you're thriving, and where a gentle recalibration might help.

We often hear "be kind to yourself," but in practice, that can feel abstract, especially when you're stretched thin. Fatherhood isn't about perfection. It's about presence. It's about noticing when you're overwhelmed, speaking it aloud, and turning toward what really matters.

Resilience isn't built in calm. It's cultivated in the mess. Through small practices: a moment of quiet, a walk, a deep breath, a check-in, a hard conversation. Fathers who prioritise mindfulness, self-care, and support, whether from partners, peers, or professionals are better equipped to ride the waves. Not because they've eliminated struggle, but because they've learned how to steady themselves within it.

## Employee benefits

Employers play a pivotal role in shaping how fathers navigate the balance between work and family life. This evolving social landscape where parenting is increasingly seen as a shared endeavour has been transformative, opening space for fathers to take a more active, present role in raising their children.

Across industries, organisations are responding. Policies that support work-life balance such as paid parental leave, flexible scheduling, and remote work options are becoming more common. These frameworks signal an important shift: that being a devoted father and a committed professional are no longer mutually exclusive identities.

And yet, the numbers in Australia paint a different picture. Only 1 in 20 fathers take on primary parental leave, and while more employers now offer paid leave, only 12% of those who use it are fathers. The gap between intention and action is often shaped by deeply embedded barriers like traditional gender roles, workplace stigma, and very real financial constraints. Many fathers want to take leave, but fear they'll be judged, overlooked, or left behind professionally.

*Finding Fatherhood* is about rebalancing these scales. It's about recognising that engaged fatherhood isn't just a private decision, it's a collective opportunity. When employers create environments that support fathers through policy, culture, and example, they help cultivate a workforce that is more loyal, motivated, and aligned.

Because when fathers feel empowered to show up fully at home, they're better equipped to show up fully at work. The result is not a loss of productivity but a redefinition of it

## Reflective Questions

Take the time to reflect on these questions:

1. Where in your life do you feel pulled in two directions?
2. How do you define balance for yourself—and how realistic does that feel right now?
3. What small changes could help you feel more present at home and in your work?

# Facing the Fear

*"There's always this little voice – am I enough for them?"*

For all its joy and meaning, fatherhood can also surface moments of profound doubt and quiet fear. From the instant a man learns he is going to be a father, questions begin to emerge:

"Will I be a good dad?"

"What if I fail my child?"

"Will be able to even settle them to sleep?"

These questions don't arrive once and quietly fade. They linger. They resurface in moments of stress like when you're running on little sleep, navigating tension at home, or walking into a meeting underprepared and out of sync if your colleagues. Alongside parenting doubts come professional ones:

"Am I letting my team down?"

"Can I actually balance all this?"

"Are my colleagues quietly questioning my priorities?"

This internal dialogue is not a sign that you're failing. It's a sign that you care deeply. And yet, without acknowledgment and support, these thoughts can quietly erode your confidence. Left unchecked, they fuel a spiral of inadequacy, frustration, and guilt. These are feelings experienced by fathers across industries, cultures, and seniority levels.

This chapter exists to name those fears. To shed light on the myths that amplify them. And to offer tools to move through them, not with perfection, but with presence. Because doubt is part of the journey. And working through it is part of becoming the father you hope to be.

## Letting go of comparisons

In the age of social media, comparison is an ever-present temptation. The dad-blogger, the influencer, even your mate down the street may appear to have parenting all figured out or at least playing out like a serene, well-edited stroll through the parklands of fatherhood. And even when you know that what you're seeing is curated, it can still feel like you're falling short.

But one of the great truths is this: we're all figuring it out. Most of us are quietly navigating our own doubts, frustrations, and trial-and-error moments. We're doing the best we can with the tools, support, and energy available to us.

That's why it's so essential to turn down the volume on comparison and tune into your own journey. Accept advice as just that: advice, not gospel. What works beautifully for one family might not serve yours, and that doesn't mean you're doing it wrong. It means you're doing it your way.

When fathers let go of the pressure to measure up and begin to trust their instincts, they create something far more powerful than perfection, they create authenticity. An environment of love, flexibility, and presence that evolves with their child's needs.

Because in the end, your child doesn't need a picture-perfect version of fatherhood, they need you. Fully engaged, constantly learning, and bravely showing up.

## Roots of doubt

Doubt in fatherhood often stems from deeply ingrained societal expectations, personal insecurities, and the sheer unpredictability of the journey ahead. Traditionally, the role of a father has been defined by strength, provision, and unshakable confidence. While these traits can be admirable, they also create a narrow, often unattainable standard that leaves many fathers silently wrestling with self-doubt when they feel they don't measure up.

Self-doubt isn't new. It has echoed across generations. What matters most is how you respond to it. How you choose to grow from it rather than let it shape your self-worth or cloud your judgment.

For some fathers, that doubt is rooted in childhood. Memories of emotionally distant, distracted, or absent fathers weigh heavily, especially for those determined to offer something different to their own children. Breaking those patterns takes more than intention. It calls for reflection. Sometimes forgiveness. And often the courage to create a new model of parenting, one shaped by your own values, not your past. In some cases, seeking professional support is an essential and healing part of that process.

For many fathers, doubt isn't just about competence, it's about identity. Becoming a father demands a shift in priorities, routines, and, perhaps most profoundly, self-perception. The transition from not being responsible for a child to caring for a fragile, developing life is abrupt and consuming, even for those who believed themselves "prepared".

The weight of this new responsibility, the maturity it requires, the constant vigilance, the tenderness and terror of holding something so vulnerable can feel overwhelming. And within that overwhelm, a quieter emotion may begin to stir: grief.

Not grief in the tragic sense, but a subtle mourning for your previous life. A life where your choices felt lighter, your movements more spontaneous, and your time (while never entirely your own) was shaped more by want than by obligation. Suddenly, your days are tethered to routines, your freedoms negotiated, and your actions shrouded with consequence.

This mourning is natural. And naming it doesn't make you ungrateful, it makes you honest. Because becoming a father doesn't erase who you were. It expands you. And sometimes, expansion feels a lot like "undoing" before it feels like "becoming".

If these doubts aren't acknowledged, they can harden into self-criticism, frustration, or resentment, at work, at home, or toward the very identity of fatherhood itself.

But naming the doubt is the first act of strength. And meeting it with curiosity, compassion, and support can transform it into one of fatherhood's most powerful growth frontiers.

## Myths that fuel fears

Over generations, myths about fatherhood have taken root in pop culture, storytelling, and even casual conversation. Films, books, and social expectations have shaped the image of what a "real father" should be, often reinforcing ideals that are unrealistic or narrow. While some of these portrayals offer meaningful models or help break harmful cycles, many perpetuate feelings of inadequacy and fear.

*"Fear used to paralyse me. Now I see it as a sign I care deeply."*

These myths don't just influence what others expect of fathers, they shape how fathers see themselves. By identifying and challenging these narratives, you create space to rewrite your own definition of fatherhood, one that is grounded in presence, growth, and authenticity.

*Myth 1:* Good fathers have all the answers...

*Reality:* No parent has all the answers and that's not only okay, it's essential. Fatherhood is a process of learning, adapting, and evolving. When you're honest about uncertainty, you foster trust with your partner and children. You teach your child that not knowing isn't weakness, it's curiosity, humility, and growth.

*Myth 2:* Fatherhood should come naturally...

*Reality:* While some moments may feel instinctive, most of fatherhood is learned through trial, error, and intention. Expecting it to "just happen" creates shame when it doesn't. Parenting is a skill, not a genetic preset, and every attempt is part of the journey.

*Myth 3:* Fathers must always be strong...

*Reality:* The pressure to be emotionally and physically strong at all times discourages vulnerability and connection. Real strength lies in openness. A father who shares his feelings and seeks help isn't weak, he's modelling resilience, emotional intelligence, and trust.

*Myth 4*: A father's worth is defined by his income or job title...

*Reality:* The narrative of the "provider" can create deep self-doubt, especially when work is precarious or overwhelming. But what your child remembers won't be your salary. It will be your laughter, your listening, your love. Presence is more powerful than a payslip.

## Navigating doubts and fears

As you face your own doubts and fears, you also hold the opportunity to reshape what fatherhood means. To rewrite the narrative in a way that reflects your values, your vulnerabilities, and your vision for what comes next. By challenging outdated myths, embracing uncertainty, and seeking support when it's needed, you begin to turn these very doubts into stepping stones like markers of growth, not setbacks.

Fatherhood isn't about eliminating doubt. It's about learning to walk with it. To navigate each moment with reflection, persistence, and a growing trust in yourself. Because fear isn't failure. It's an invitation: to grow deeper, love harder, and live more fully in each passing season.

This journey will ask tough questions of you. And it will gift you the strength to answer them, not always perfectly, but honestly. And in doing so, you create a legacy of love, resilience, and presence that lives on in your child long after the doubts have faded.

That's what makes you a capable father. Not certainty. But courage.

## Learning from vulnerability

One of the most powerful antidotes to doubt is vulnerability. Naming your fears, exploring where they come from, asking for help, and opening up emotionally. These are not signs of weakness, they are acts of extraordinary courage.

In recent years, society has begun to reframe vulnerability as a strength, especially for men. While the image of the stoic, emotionally distant father still lingers in parts of culture, there has been a profound shift. A growing understanding of mental health and emotional wellbeing is helping to dismantle long-held stereotypes that have limited boys and men for generations.

When fathers lead with vulnerability, they do more than model emotional intelligence, they create a safe space. A space where children learn that their feelings are valid. Where they see that struggle is part of life, and that asking for help is not only acceptable, but wise. By sharing challenges and regulating your emotions in real time, you teach your child how to do the same. Ultimately, building resilience, empathy, and trust in the process.

*"There are days I question if I'm doing any of it right. But I keep showing up—and maybe that's enough."*

This is the emotional scaffolding of fatherhood. The deep work that isn't always visible, but profoundly felt. And over time, it becomes the foundation of a bond strong enough to hold whatever the unpredictability of life might bring.

## Reframing fear as growth

Stepping into the unknown is one of life's most fear-inducing experiences. And few unknowns carry the emotional weight of becoming a father. While the idea of fatherhood may feel somewhat familiar as it has been shaped by your own experiences with dads, father figures, or friends stepping into the role, the deeper uncertainty lies in a far more personal question: "Will I be a good father?"

This isn't a question about bottles or bedtime routines. It's about something much deeper: the fear of failure. Put simply, not living up to the responsibility now placed in your hands. Because in an instant, your decisions, your presence, your energy, your love, all carry weight not just for you, but for someone else.

Every father's experience with this fear is different. Some feel it quietly creep in. Others feel it hit like a wave. But it almost always ignites the same deep shift: the realisation that you are now responsible for another life. And that responsibility brings an emotional weight no one can fully prepare you for.

What's even more daunting is that you don't yet know how you will respond. There will be countless firsts, some magical, others disorienting. And many of them will arrive when you're sleep-deprived, emotionally stretched, and questioning if you're getting any of it right.

But that question: "Will I be a good father?" isn't a sign of doubt. It's a sign of devotion. The fact that you're asking it at all means you're already becoming the kind of father your child will be proud of.

Fear can overwhelm. It can freeze you in place, whispering that you're not ready, not capable, not enough. But when you begin to recognise fear as something that rises from within, often not to stop you, but a signal for growth, you gain the power to reframe it. To see it not as a threat, but as an opportunity.

Fatherhood is one of life's greatest invitations to step beyond the familiar. It will push you beyond your comfort zones, your certainty, your well-worn routines. And it is precisely in that unfamiliar space, where your footing is unsure and your heart is wide open, that real growth happens.

*"I didn't grow up with a good example, so I question everything I do."*

This is the power of a growth mindset. It allows you to meet each challenge not with perfection, but with curiosity. Not with shame, but with willingness. It transforms fear from a stop sign into a guidepost. A reminder that something meaningful is unfolding.

Mistakes will happen. That's not a flaw in the process. It is the process. What matters is how you respond: by pausing, reflecting, learning, and trying again.

Because with every stumble, every try, and every small step forward, you become not a perfect father, but a growing one. And that, more than anything, is what your child needs as they grow.

## The courage to show up

Courage is often confused with bravery. But at its root, courage comes from the Latin *cor*—meaning "heart." To live courageously is to live wholeheartedly: with commitment, resolve, and the strength to keep showing up, even (and especially) when it's hard.

That's what fatherhood demands. Not fearlessness, but presence. Not perfection, but perseverance. It's choosing to stand in the gap between fear and love and say: "I'm here anyway".

Finding the courage to show up, despite doubts, missteps, and moments of exhaustion is the essence of being a father. It's a testament to your resilience and love, and it's what shapes the connection that lasts long after the sleepless nights and chaotic mornings fade.

Yes, the fears may linger. The questions may return. But they do not define your worth, your capacity, or your ability to love well.

What matters most is your willingness: to stay engaged, to keep learning, and to nurture a space where your child can grow.

Because fatherhood isn't about having all the answers. It's about choosing, again and again, to live with your heart wide open.

## The role of community

As men move through different life stages, friendships often fade quietly into the background. It's rarely intentional. Life just happens, workplaces change, people move, team sports get shelved, new relationships or routines take priority, and before long, the rhythm that sustained our social connections begins to shift.

A significant catalyst for this evolution is entering a new 'phase' of life like becoming a parent. When you have a baby, your priorities naturally change. Suddenly, late nights out and spontaneous plans don't align with nap schedules, bedtime routines, or the sheer exhaustion that accompanies early parenthood. And if your friends aren't in the same phase, it can feel like you're speaking different languages entirely.

Yet even as friendships shift, the need for community becomes more important, not less. Building a support network plays a vital role in providing perspective, encouragement, and reassurance. Whether it's through local parenting groups, online communities, or casual backyard catch-ups with fellow dads, these conversations remind you that you're not alone.

Community also creates space to share stories, swap ideas, and learn from others' experiences. It invites vulnerability, laughter, and solidarity in the face of shared uncertainty. And perhaps most powerfully, it reminds us that doubt, fear, and joy are part of a universal fatherhood story. One that grows stronger each time it's told out loud.

# Reflective Questions

Take the time to reflect on these questions:

1. What is one fear about fatherhood you've carried that you've never said out loud?
2. How do you normally respond to self-doubt as a parent?
3. What would it mean to give yourself permission to grow and learn through mistakes?

# Art of Being Present

*"You can't outsource presence – it's about being emotionally available, not just physically there."*

Saying "life is busy" almost feels like both an understatement and a deflection. Everyone seems to be under the pump with juggling work, relationships, commitments or just trying to keep their head above water. The sheer volume of competing demands leaves little space for a sense of mastery, completion, or even competence.

In this whirlwind, the act of being truly present has become a rare skill and a foundational element of fatherhood.

Presence isn't loud. It doesn't come from grand gestures or declarations like "I'm here for you". It lives in the small, intentional moments shared, like kneeling down to tie a shoe, asking a follow-up question at dinner, or grabbing an extra book to read at bedtime. These are the moments that deepen connection and create lasting impressions.

Being physically available is one thing. But being mentally and emotionally with your child? Well, that's another level and a much harder one to access when your mind is fractured by deadlines, stress, or fatigue. Your ability to be present, like any discipline, will shift. It will get tested. It may feel impossible at times.

But the pursuit matters. Because in those fleeting moments when your attention aligns with your child's world, something powerful happens. Not productivity. Not efficiency. Something better: belonging.

And to your child, those moments are everything.

## Why presence matters

Presence is the cornerstone of connection. Children, no matter their age, yearn for their parents' attention and engagement. It's through consistent presence that fathers build trust, nurture open communication, and create a deep sense of safety and belonging. When a father shows up, fully and without distraction, he sends an unspoken but powerful message: "You matter to me. I see you. I value you".

For generations, the dominant belief was that a father's primary role was to provide financially. While that contribution is undeniably important, it has often come at the expense of emotional connection. This mindset sidelined many fathers' own desires to engage more deeply, and equally devalued their child's innate need to feel emotionally close to their dad, not just taken care of, but known and loved.

Thankfully, these views are shifting. As society begins to place greater emphasis on emotional wellbeing, we're also seeing a growing recognition of the father's role in nurturing it. Emotional presence is now understood not as an optional bonus, but as an essential foundation for a child's development.

*"I worry they'll grow up remembering a distracted version of me."*

Today, there is a powerful invitation for fathers to show up, not just as providers, but as active participants in their children's lives. And in doing so, they not only strengthen the parent-child bond, but they also redefine what it means to be a dad for themselves, their families, and importantly the next generation.

Being present is often easier said than done. In the blur of modern life, full attention (physical and emotional) can feel like a luxury. But presence is more than proximity. It's the practice of engaging in the moment without distraction, truly listening to understand, and responding with care, curiosity, and connection.

Being present means:

- **Putting away distractions:** Letting that message or email wait so your child gets your full focus.
- **Listening without interruption:** Giving your child space to finish their thought, however meandering or slow.
- **Supporting emotion with empathy:** Meeting your child's feelings with patience, encouragement, and a steady calm.
- **Slowing down:** Taking a beat to celebrate a moment, a drawing, a question, a shared laugh, without rushing off to the next thing.

And this isn't just feel-good advice. Research backs it. Studies consistently show that children with present and engaged parents' experience higher self-esteem, stronger emotional regulation, and better communication and social skills.

But presence does more than foster development, it creates memories. Memories your child will carry into adulthood. It shapes how they give and receive love, how they handle stress, and how they show up in their own relationships.

And in the process of showing up for your child, you may just find yourself more anchored too. More connected not only to them, but to a deeper version of yourself.

## The challenges of being present

Despite its importance, being present is not always easy. No doubt you face numerous challenges that can pull you away from the moment.

In a world shaped by smartphones, emails, and always-on social media, attention has become a precious and fragile currency. The pull of constant connectivity often blurs the line between work and home, making it difficult to fully switch off and engage in family life.

For many fathers, this creates a quiet but persistent dilemma. Even when physically present, their minds may still be tethered to inboxes, news feeds, or the gnawing sense of something left undone. The result is a subtle yet powerful barrier between themselves and their children, a disconnect that can erode opportunities for meaningful interaction.

It's not a question of care or intent. It's a reflection of the digital age we live in. And yet, recognising this dynamic is the first step toward change.

Because presence doesn't just happen. It's created, moment-by-moment by choosing to close the laptop, silence the notifications, and turn toward what truly matters. And in doing so, fathers affirm something that no message or alert could ever replace: "you are more important than anything happening on this screen".

## Work life balance

High-demand careers often require long hours, regular travel, and after-hours commitments that leave little space for home life. And even when you are physically present, the mental load of work can follow you through the door, quietly colouring the moments that should feel light, joyful, or restful.

You may find yourself replaying difficult conversations, troubleshooting tomorrow's deadlines, or mentally walking through next week's agenda while sitting at the dinner table or tucking your child into bed. These moments, meant for connection, can feel dulled by a brain that's still at work.

This is the paradox of modern fatherhood: striving to be present while pulled by the unfinished business of the day. It's not a reflection of carelessness or imbalance, it's a reflection of how much you care, in all directions.

The challenge isn't just time management. It's attention management. And learning to reclaim even a few moments of mental clarity, whether through simple transitions, digital detoxes, or mindful breathing, can begin to rewire your ability to return, again and again, to what is in front of you.

## Emotional fatigue

The stresses of life like financial strain, relationship tensions, personal uncertainty, can quietly erode our emotional reserves. And when energy runs low, even the most cherished parenting moments can begin to feel like chores to complete, rather than experiences to embrace.

Emotional fatigue has a subtle way of creating detachment. You might be sitting beside your child, reading their favourite bedtime story, but your mind is somewhere else entirely, replaying difficult meetings, worrying about tomorrow's deadlines, or simply counting down to the next obligation. You're there in body, but not in spirit.

When you catch yourself, this disconnect can be disheartening. Not because you don't care, but because you actually care and wish you had more to give.

But presence doesn't require perfection. It requires noticing. The moment you become aware that you're drifting, you can gently redirect your attention. A deep breath. A reminder of what this moment means.

A simple, quiet return to your child's world, even if only for a few seconds.

Because for your child, those seconds count. Even a small moment of genuine connection like a simple smile, a question, a hand resting calmly on theirs, can anchor them. And, perhaps unexpectedly, anchor you too.

## Perfectionism and pressure

Many fathers carry the weight of perfection. The quiet pressure to always respond with wisdom, stay calm under stress, or make every interaction meaningful. But that pressure, while born from care, can quietly erode the ability to be present.

Perfectionism breeds unrealistic expectations. It insists that parenting should be poetic, that each moment with your child must be profound or picture-perfect. And when reality doesn't match the ideal, when you fumble a bedtime story, lose your temper, or forget something important, it can trigger waves of guilt, self-doubt, and distress.

> *"My father wasn't perfect, but he showed up. That's what I carry with me."*

The irony is that in striving to be the perfect dad, you can begin to miss the dad your child needs most: the one who's real, human, and emotionally available.

Presence doesn't demand perfection. It asks for honesty. For attention. For the courage to show up, flawed and tired, and still choose connection. Because the moments that matter most are often quiet and imperfect like finding the largest leaf in the park, sitting beside them during a tantrum, or laughing at a silly joke. These are the spaces where trust and love flourish.

Letting go of perfection opens space for joy, for growth, for the freedom to learn together.

## The myth of multitasking

In the scramble to meet all the demands of work, home, and parenthood, many fathers fall into the belief that they need to be everywhere at once. But the reality is that multitasking often comes at a cost: the depth of connection in any one moment begins to fade. When attention is split between playtime and emails, TV and dinner, bedtime routines and tomorrow's to-do list, children can be left feeling unseen and unheard.

And the impact isn't just on them. That fragmented presence can leave you feeling like you're failing on all fronts: never doing enough, never doing it well, and never quite being the father you want to be.

The truth is, distraction erodes not just efficiency, but intimacy. And while life may always be full, the quality of your attention is what truly matters. Because when you're fully present, even for a few moments, you give your child something invaluable: a deep sense of worth, belonging, and love.

And for you? Those moments offer something in return. A sense of fulfillment, of capability, and of genuine connection that no checklist can replace.

## Techniques for cultivating presence

While you may want the ability to be present and in the moment with your child at every interaction, the challenges affecting your ability to achieve this are numerous and real. However, there are practical strategies that fathers can use to cultivate presence and create meaningful connections with their children. These strategies are a combination of establishing approaches or systems to create the ability to focus in the moment, and a shift in mindset and how you value your time.

## Prioritise quality over quantity

Presence isn't measured by the number of hours you spend with your child; it's defined by the quality of the moments you share. A 15-minute conversation filled with curiosity, or a burst of distraction-free play, can leave a deeper imprint than an entire day spent half-engaged.

It's about depth, not duration.

These moments of focused attention may happen before you head out the door for work, or in the quiet after dinner, but whenever they arise, they send a powerful message: "You matter. I see you. I care".

> *"Just being with them—watching, listening, holding—it's where I feel most alive."*

In the rush of daily life, it's easy to underestimate the impact of these small acts. But for a child, they are anchors shaping their confidence, their sense of belonging, and their belief that they are worthy of love and attention.

And for fathers, these moments don't just build connection, they build legacy.

## Create rituals and routines

Rituals offer structured, reliable opportunities for presence. Whether it's reading a bedtime story, taking a weekend hike, or sitting down for nightly family dinner, these repeated moments become anchors of connection. For children, rituals offer predictability. A comforting rhythm in a world that often feels fast and unpredictable. For fathers, they provide a built-in rhythm for showing up and tuning in.

These moments don't need to be elaborate to be meaningful. In fact, it's the consistency that counts. Rituals like a shared meal, a Saturday morning walk, or a pre-bed chat at lights out can become sacred ground for connection, where love is communicated not just in words, but in routine and presence.

Setting boundaries around these moments strengthens them. That might mean creating a no-phone zone at the dinner table, choosing a nightly game that encourages sharing, or simply turning off notifications during play. These small shifts create powerful messages: "You matter more than my inbox. This time is ours".

Over time, rituals and boundaries together do more than reduce distraction. They nurture trust, model healthy communication, and offer both you and your child a steady place to return to again and again.

## Practicing Mindfulness

Mindfulness is the practice of being fully present: right here, right now and without judgment or distraction. For fathers, it can be a powerful tool for reconnecting in the midst of chaos, exhaustion, or emotional fog.

Simple techniques like deep breathing or grounding exercises can bring your attention back to the moment. Not the imagined future or the unfinished task list, but this moment unfolding in front of you.

Mindfulness invites you to slow down. To notice your child's laughter, the tilt of their head, the way their fingers curl around yours. These small details are easy to overlook, but they are the heartbeat of connection. They remind you that presence isn't something you chase. It's something you choose.

Practicing mindfulness daily, whether through intentional breathing, meditation, or simply quiet observation—doesn't just help in the moment. It builds an overarching sense of gratitude, calm, and emotional resilience. Over time, it can become a steadying force. One that helps you meet stress with patience, respond rather than react, and feel more grounded in both fatherhood and life.

## Set boundaries with technology

Limiting screen time and setting boundaries for work tasks are powerful ways to protect family moments and prioritise connection. In a world where devices constantly call for your attention, creating intentional space to step away is both restorative and deeply relational.

Designating tech-free times like family dinners or bedtime routines, establishes a shared agreement that this time is sacred. These boundaries help children feel seen and valued, while reinforcing the idea that connection is worth protecting.

Practical strategies might include:

1. Leaving phones in another room during meals or play
2. Turning off non-essential notifications in the evenings
3. Setting calendar blocks for family time so they're visible (and respected)
4. Creating "do not disturb" rituals for transition periods, like coming home from work
5. Communicating with colleagues about your boundaries so

expectations are clear and sustainable

These practices not only make your time with your children more meaningful, they also model digital discipline, emotional availability, and champions what it looks like to value relationships over reactions.

Over time, these small shifts don't just support your presence, they support your peace.

## Engage active listening

Modelling positive communication isn't just about the words you use with your children or partner, it's also about how you listen. Being present means going beyond simply hearing. It means truly listening.

This kind of listening is active, intentional, and full of care. It involves:

- Making eye contact that says, "I'm here and you have my full attention."
- Asking open-ended questions that invite your child to share what they're thinking and feeling.
- Validating emotions, even when they're uncomfortable, offering responses like "I can see that really upset you" or "That makes sense you'd feel that way."

When fathers listen this way, it builds more than conversation, it builds trust. It shows children that their thoughts matter, their feelings are valid, and they are safe to express themselves.

And over time, these small acts of listening become some of the most powerful lessons a child learns: that connection starts with curiosity, and caring sounds a lot like "tell me more."

## Embrace playfulness

Children have an innate and endless desire to explore, and play is their natural language. Whether it's building a Duplo castle, wandering through a local park, or turning the lounge room into a blanket fort, play sparks imagination, deepens joy, and forges powerful bonds between father and child.

Play also offers something extraordinary: the chance for fathers to connect on their child's level. It invites you to set aside the role of authority, even for just a moment, and step into a shared space of curiosity, creativity, and silliness. In these moments, laughter becomes a bridge. And the stresses of the day, the worries of work, the fatigue of parenting, they can melt away, even if just for a while.

*"My son doesn't remember the gifts. He remembers when I sat on the floor and played trucks with him."*

These aren't just fun moments. They are formative ones. Joyful play creates memories that children carry with them, not just of what you did together, but of how they felt with you: safe, loved, and free to be themselves.

Cultivating presence through play doesn't require perfection or hours of free time. It begins with intention, with creating systems that allow you to pause, shift focus, and join your child in their world. It also requires mindset to approach a moment not as a task, but as a gift.

And in doing so, you don't just help your child grow and explore. You grow too. More connected, more fulfilled, and more the father you want to be.

## Overcoming barriers to presence

Even with the best intentions, setbacks are inevitable. Life will test your ability to be physically and emotionally present. Especially, with work demands, fatigue, unexpected obligations, or emotional overwhelm pulling you in different directions.

Some barriers will be out of your control. Others may be self-imposed. But presence doesn't require perfection, it requires honesty. Being able to notice when you're not fully there, name the challenge, and gently course-correct is one of the most important skills a father can cultivate.

Striving for quality over quantity means learning to make the most of the moments you do have. That begins with acknowledging the barriers, whether they're time, energy, stress, or mindset, and building strategies to meet them with intention.

Even small actions like a shift in schedule, a tech-free window, a moment of emotional check-in can help you hold space for connection, even amidst life's chaos.

Because presence isn't just about showing up. It's about showing up with awareness. And that mindset alone can transform how you connect, how you recover from setbacks, and how your child experiences your love, even in the busiest seasons.

## Recognise triggers

Presence begins with awareness and that means noticing the moments, patterns, or stressors that consistently pull you away from connection. These triggers may look different for every father. For some, it's the mental weight of work: unresolved tasks, difficult conversations, or looming deadlines. For others, it's more internal like personal insecurities, perfectionism, or the fear of not being enough.

The key is not to eliminate these triggers but to name them.

Self-reflection tools like journaling can help uncover the moments when presence feels hardest. What time of day are you most distracted? What emotions tend to shut you down? Are there specific activities or conversations that spike your stress levels?

Once identified, these triggers lose some of their power. You begin to recognise them not as character flaws, but as signals. Opportunities to respond differently next time. Over time, this awareness becomes a kind of emotional muscle memory. It allows you to pause, recalibrate, and return to the moment with greater intention and grace.

Because the more clearly you understand what pulls you away, the more equipped you are to find your way back

## Seek support

Fatherhood can be one of life's most enriching journeys and one of its most daunting, especially for first-time fathers. The weight of new responsibilities, identity shifts, and constant learning can feel overwhelming. But the truth is, you don't have to carry it all alone.

Leaning on your partner, family, friends, or support networks isn't a sign of weakness, it's a sign of wisdom. Talking through challenges, dividing responsibilities, and asking for guidance can ease the emotional load and create the space you need to be present. These conversations often bring unexpected perspective, reassurance, or even a moment of much-needed laughter.

Support also comes from recognising when you're not okay. If stress, anxiety, or emotional exhaustion begin to impact your wellbeing, it's important to reach out to a trusted friend, a counsellor, or a psychologist. Professional support doesn't mean something is broken. It means you care enough to look after yourself so you can keep showing up for the people who matter most.

Because presence begins with you. And staying connected to others and to yourself is not just part of the journey. It is the journey.

## Practice self-care

It begins with wellbeing. Fathers who care for their physical, emotional, and mental health are far better equipped to show up fully and consistently for their children, their partners, and their work.

Establishing a routine that includes regular movement, quality sleep, nourishing meals, and space for personal interests helps recharge your energy and sharpen your focus. These aren't luxuries. They're investments in your capacity to engage, connect, and parent with intention.

There may be moments when taking time for yourself stirs guilt. But self-care is not time away from your family, it's time that strengthens your ability to be there in the ways that matter most.

When you're rested, centred, and emotionally grounded, you're not just more efficient. You're more patient, more joyful, more present. And that version of you (the one who's fuelled rather than depleted) is a gift not only to yourself, but to everyone you love.

## The ripple effect of presence

The power of presence extends far beyond the moments you share with your child today. When fathers show up with intention and modelling active listening, empathy, and emotional availability, they create ripples that shape a child's world in lasting, often unseen ways.

These ripples influence how children relate to others, how they handle challenges, and how deeply they believe they are worthy of love and connection. Presence is not just a gift in the moment, it's an investment in the future.

Here are just a few of the ways those ripples move outward:

1. **Building trust**: Consistent presence creates the foundation for open communication and mutual respect. When children feel truly seen and heard, they're more likely to turn to their fathers for guidance, especially during life's most complex moments.
2. **Fostering emotional intelligence**: Through presence, fathers' model emotional awareness, mindfulness, and active listening. Skills that their children will carry into friendships, future relationships, and leadership roles for years to come.
3. **Creating lasting memories**: The simple moments like shared laughter, quiet bedtime chats, unstructured play become anchors in a child's memory. These memories shape how they view their father, their family, and their own sense of value.
4. **Strengthening family bonds**: Presence cultivates a sense of safety and belonging that holds families together. It reinforces the message: "We're in this together. We choose each other, every day".

The importance of presence cannot be overstated. It is the foundation of meaningful relationships, the bridge between intention and connection, and the most enduring gift a father can give.

The demands of modern life may make it difficult to be fully present, but it is always worth striving for. Presence only for your authenticity, your attention, and your love.

As you walk the path of fatherhood, remember: it's not about grand gestures or flawless execution. It's about being there in the small, everyday moments that quietly stitch together a lifetime. One interaction. One conversation. One shared laugh at a time.

Presence is the greatest act of love. It tells your children, "You matter. You are seen. You are loved." And long after the moments have passed, what remains is a sense of connection that they will carry forward into their own relationships, their own challenges, their own lives.

Because in the end, they may not remember every word you said. But they will remember how it felt to be with you.

# Reflective Questions

Take the time to reflect on these questions:

1. When was the last time you felt truly present with your child or partner?
2. What tends to distract you most from being mentally and emotionally available?
3. What would it look like to be more present, even for just 10 minutes a day?

# The Wisdom Collective

*"Mentorship changed me. I saw what fatherhood could look like beyond my own experience."*

Our understanding of fatherhood is rarely built in isolation. It's shaped by those who came before us, the good, the flawed, the devoted, and the distant. Parents, mentors, coaches, family members; these role models leave behind impressions, stories, and lessons that become the scaffolding for how we show up in our own parenting.

Sometimes these figures inspire imitation, offering a clear picture of the kind of father we hope to be. Other times, they spark a determination to do things differently. Either way, no one walks into fatherhood untouched by influence.

Each of us is part of a larger, ongoing story, like an endless chain of parental influence. As fathers, we're both recipients and contributors. We inherit and we pass on. Our presence, our choices, our growth all ripple forward into the lives of our children, shaping how they see the world, how they treat others, and how they one day may parent themselves.

The wisdom collective lives in us. And as we draw from it we build on our strengths, heal from our wounds, reshape what needs to be reimagined, and ultimately become an intentional thread in the fabric of future generations.

## The legacy of parental figures

For many fathers, their own parents serve as their first and most enduring role models. These early experiences, whether nurturing or neglectful, empowering or painful, leave powerful impressions. Consciously or unconsciously, they shape our expectations, inform our values, and guide us on the parenting road ahead.

Fathers often find themselves drawing lessons from how they were raised:

- The warmth they want to replicate.
- The patterns they hope to improve.
- The wounds they're determined not to pass on.

But this legacy is not a fixed blueprint. It's a starting point. And the task is not to copy or reject the past in full but to wrestle with it, learn from it, and carry forward only what serves your child's growth and your own integrity.

Importantly, these lessons are not static. As fathers grow through reflection, through feedback, through the lived experience of raising children, their approach continues to evolve. The version of fatherhood you live out today may differ from the one you carry forward tomorrow. And that adaptability is not a weakness. It's wisdom.

You are not just the product of those who came before. You are a contributor to what comes next. And through presence, reflection, and love, you can shape a legacy your child will someday be proud to inherit.

## Lessons learned

As you navigate the early days of fatherhood, your lived experience will often challenge the expectations you once held. Many fathers come to realise that their assumptions about who they'd be, how they'd feel, or what parenthood "should" look like are reshaped by the beautiful, unpredictable reality of raising a child.

One of the most liberating lessons...? Children are incredibly resilient. They don't need perfect parents. They need present, loving ones. This truth can free fathers from the impossible pressures of perfection, often amplified by social media, to allow them to focus on what truly matters: connection, care, and showing up, even imperfectly.

Another profound lesson is the importance of flexibility. Children grow and change with stunning speed, and what works today might be entirely irrelevant tomorrow. Fathers who embrace curiosity and adaptability rather than clinging to control, often find the journey more joyful, less anxiety-provoking, and full of unexpected magic. No matter how brilliant yesterday was, each day asks for a fresh approach. And no matter how hard today feels, tomorrow invites you to begin again.

Building a support network is not a luxury, it's a lifeline. Whether through family, friends, or community groups, seeking out others who walk a similar path can offer reassurance and wisdom. Sharing stories of missteps, of triumphs, of tender surprises, reminds fathers they're not alone. And in a world that is (finally) beginning to take men's mental health seriously, the importance of connection and emotional support is a welcome and vital shift.

## Reaching out to mentors

While our parents often provide the initial blueprint, many of the most transformative insights into fatherhood come from outside that foundation. External mentors like family friends, coaches, teachers, colleagues, even admired public figures, offer fresh perspectives, objective guidance, and lived wisdom that stretch our understanding of what's possible.

These mentors often model not just "what" to do, but "how" to be, providing examples that bring to life values like leadership, compassion, integrity, and emotional presence. Their influence often transcends parenting techniques, encouraging deeper questions like:

> "What kind of father do I want to be?"
>
> "How do I balance my ambitions with my relationships?"
>
> "What legacy am I quietly shaping, moment by moment?"

In the professional sphere, the rise of executive coaching speaks to this need for holistic support. While often tied to career growth, many executive coaches approach their work with an understanding that no part of your life exists in isolation. They help fathers navigate the demands of work, relationships, identity, and purpose, offering tools to clarify priorities, manage time and stress, and build a life aligned with deeper values.

Mentorship, at its best, offers more than solutions. It offers space to reflect, to question, to evolve. And in the journey of fatherhood, that space can be the difference between running on autopilot and parenting with intention.

Because when we surround ourselves with people who challenge, support, and inspire us, we don't just grow. We model growth for our children, teaching them by example how to seek wisdom, embrace change, and become lifelong learners. Engaging an external mentor offers more than advice, it provides a safe space for self-discovery. In the day-to-day demands of fatherhood, career, and personal growth, it's easy to lose sight of your own aspirations. Mentors create room to pause, explore, and refocus.

They help break down the pressure points like the relentless pulls on your time, energy, and attention. They can help you spot the difference between a real limitation and a perceived one. And most importantly, they support you in articulating what truly matters, so that your path reflects your values, not just your responsibilities.

---

*"I had no one to model myself on. I'm building something I never saw growing up."*

---

This process of introspection is not one-size-fits-all. Whether it's through conversation, journaling, structured exercises, or simple reflection, mentors guide fathers in finding their own rhythms or the pathways that suit their unique circumstances and the season of life they're in.

What makes mentors especially powerful is their duality:

- They offer reassurance and lived wisdom, helping you feel seen and less alone.
- They provide objectivity and honest perspective, helping you challenge assumptions and grow.

Unlike parental figures, whose influence is often bound in emotion and memory, mentors bring a clarity that's refreshingly grounding. They see you not through the lens of your past, but through the promise of who you're becoming.

And in the journey of fatherhood, that clarity can be transformative, not just for you, but for the child watching you learn, grow, and lead with intention.

## The influence of community

Community isn't just defined by proximity or shared memberships, it's about connection. It's the feeling that you're part of something larger than yourself, bound by shared purpose, history, values, or care.

Before fatherhood, that sense of belonging might have come from weekly soccer matches, late-night chats in gaming forums, dinners with old friends, or the camaraderie of a workplace team. But with the arrival of a new baby and a shift in responsibilities, that connection can quietly slip away.

This transition isn't often talked about. The demands of supporting a partner, navigating sleepless nights, and learning your new identity as a father can leave little time or energy for the people and places that once kept you grounded. You may find yourself out of rhythm with friends who are in different life stages or even grieving the version of yourself that had more space for connection.

And yet, the need for community doesn't vanish. In many ways, it grows deeper. Because while fatherhood can be a profoundly personal journey, it's not meant to be walked alone.

Recognising and naming this shift is the first step. From there, it becomes possible to rebuild community in ways that align with this new chapter, whether that's finding other parents to connect with, rekindling old friendships through new rituals, or simply allowing space for new relationships to emerge.

The shape of community may change but its importance remains. It offers support, perspective, laughter, and the quiet reminder: you are not alone.

## Generational lessons

The influence of role models reaches far beyond specific parenting techniques. It shapes how we strive for balance across work, life, and fatherhood and more deeply, how we understand character, resilience, and love. These lessons have been shaped and refined over generations, each father adapting them within the context of their time, values, and challenges.

Here are just a few enduring takeaways:

1. **Patience is a virtue**: Watching fathers who embody calm presence reminds us that composure, even in the face of chaos, builds safety and teaches children how to regulate their own emotions.
2. **Vulnerability is strength**: Fathers who show their feelings and ask for help model that emotional openness is not weakness, but courage. Their example gives children permission to do the same.
3. **Consistency builds trust**: Reliability creates security. When a father is consistent with his time, his words, and his boundaries, builds a foundation that children can stand on.
4. **Adaptability is key**: Parenting is never static. Fathers who stay flexible, curious, and responsive to change show that growth isn't just expected, it's embraced.
5. **Empathy strengthens relationships**: Seeing the world through your child's eyes nurtures a bond built on understanding. Empathy doesn't just improve connection, it deepens your influence.

Learning from role models is not a one-time inheritance. It's a lifelong evolution. As you move through different seasons of life and fatherhood, these lessons continue to take new shape. Often informing not just "how" you parent, but "who" you are becoming.

## Pass it on

At its heart, the influence of role models is about connection to our community, to those who've shaped us, and to the children we're now shaping. By reflecting on the lessons, we've learned and intentionally passing them forward, we honour the legacy of those who have guided us, whether through wisdom, example, or even through their absence.

Becoming a role model doesn't require perfection. It requires presence, authenticity, and a willingness to share what you've gained along the way. Fathers who embrace this role not only impact their own families, they help build a broader culture of engaged, compassionate parenting.

---

*"I had to look beyond my family for role models. Mentors taught me how to father by being human first."*

---

Mentoring others, either formally or informally, strengthens your own growth. It reinforces the values you hold dear and invites reflection that sharpens your path. In giving guidance, you often uncover your own.

Because fatherhood is not a solo act. It's a collective effort, carried on the shoulders of those who came before us and extended through the hands we hold now. The best we can do is listen, learn, grow and then pass it on.

# Reflective Questions

Take the time to reflect on these questions:

1. Who has been a positive role model in your life and what did they teach you?
2. What parts of your upbringing do you want to repeat? What parts do you want to leave behind?
3. How are you becoming a role model for your children?

# Rituals that Matter

*"My son knows the bedtime story is our moment. Even if I'm exhausted, I show up for that."*

Holding the tensions of family life and work commitments can feel like gripping two kites in a fierce wind. Each tugging in a different direction, unpredictable and relentless. Yet in the chaos; you are the anchor. The one who steadies, who holds fast, who keeps connection tethered to the ground.

In the swirl of a busy and often unpredictable life, building rituals and traditions becomes an anchoring practice. Offering a way to create connection, meaning, and stability for both you and your children.

Whether big or small, these rituals foster deeper bonds, create cherished memories, and pass on values that echo across generations. From weekly family dinners to bedtime routines, faith-based practices to Friday night board games, rituals become the rhythm of family life. They help children feel known, safe, and rooted in something larger than themselves.

Rituals may be shaped by culture, faith, family habits, or personal intention. But at their core, they serve the same purpose: to connect. They teach what matters most, not through lectures, but through repetition, warmth, and presence.

These simple, steady acts don't just enrich the parenting journey. They leave a legacy, one your children will carry forward in their own rhythms, one laugh, one story, one sacred moment at a time.

## Importance of rituals and traditions

In the often chaotic early years of parenthood, rituals and traditions can offer a vital sense of rhythm, stability, and meaning. Every family's rituals look different, some may gather for Friday night dinners, others for weekend bushwalks, bedtime prayers, or a beloved games-and-pizza night. These practices build continuity and create a sense of joyful anticipation. More importantly, they help children feel safe, seen, and deeply loved.

Often, these rituals are carried from our own childhoods, typically shaped by the ways our families celebrated, connected, or wound down the week. They might explain why you support a particular footy team, how you express your spirituality, or how you mark the beginning of the weekend. It's not always the activity itself that carries the meaning but the feeling it evokes. A quiet sense of belonging. A warm memory that endures.

It's also important to recognise that rituals extend beyond family togetherness. They include the practices that restore you and support your partner. A morning run, a weekly yoga class, 15 minutes for coffee and silence, these acts of self-care are more than "nice to haves." They are foundations of balance, resilience, and emotional sustainability.

---

*"I never had traditions growing up, so I'm afraid of doing it all wrong."*

---

When fathers intentionally protect time for their own wellbeing, they model self-respect, discipline, and emotional literacy for their children. These rituals don't just replenish your energy, they reinforce the message that caring for yourself is not selfish. It's essential

## Rituals in parenting

Rituals and traditions aren't just routines, they're vessels of emotional meaning, symbolic depth, and shared purpose. Unlike the logistical swirl of daily parenting, rituals are intentional moments almost like small ceremonies of connection that affirm what matters most.

In a child's unpredictable world, these rituals offer stability. They create a sense of trust, predictability, and emotional safety, forming a foundation that children lean on as they grow. Knowing what to expect, whether it's the rhythm of bedtime stories, weekend pancakes, or a simple goodbye hug, helps children feel secure and grounded.

For fathers balancing demanding careers or full schedules, these rituals become anchors. They offer intentional pauses in the rush of life, a quiet moment to reorient, reconnect, and remember who you are in your child's life. Whether five minutes or an hour, these practices communicate: "I am here. You matter."

Rituals don't require perfection or grandeur. They require presence. And that presence, repeated in meaningful ways, becomes the memory your child will carry for a lifetime.

## Faith and spirituality in family life

Faith and spirituality have long been cornerstones of family rituals, offering guidance, comfort, and a shared sense of purpose. For many fathers, faith-based practices play a vital role in parenting, creating opportunities to instil values, deepen connection, and offer a moral framework that shapes both everyday choices and lifelong beliefs.

These rituals often extend beyond formal religious observance. They become spaces to teach children about gratitude, compassion, resilience, and reverence for self, for others, and for something greater than oneself. In times of challenge or celebration, these practices provide language, structure, and meaning that anchor children in a sense of community and belonging.

---

*"Traditions give our family a rhythm. They remind us who we are, together."*

---

But faith isn't the only pathway to spirituality. For fathers who don't follow a particular religion, spirituality can still be expressed through rituals of mindfulness, gratitude, or awe. A quiet moment of reflection, a daily gratitude practice, a weekly nature walk. These acts can become sacred in their own right. They offer time to pause, connect, and reflect on what matters most.

What unites all spiritual rituals, whether rooted in faith, tradition, or intention, is the desire to connect: to values, to family, to wonder, and to something beyond the noise of daily life. In this way, spirituality becomes a quiet thread woven through the fabric of fatherhood, helping shape not just what children believe, but how they live.

## Building a legacy

Rituals and traditions are deeply personal. They often emerge slowly, shaped by the values, personalities, cultures, and beliefs that make each family unique. Whether it's a simple Friday movie night, an annual camping trip, or a moment of shared silence before dinner, what matters most isn't the activity, it's the meaning behind it: family, connection, joy, and purpose.

These traditions create continuity. They link generations, preserve shared memories, and offer children a sense of identity that they carry into adulthood. More than just routines, they become emotional landmarks. Reminders of where they come from, and what they belong to.

Often, rituals grow from the values parents hold dear. Whether it's honesty, curiosity, perseverance, or kindness, these principles take hold in the small, repeated acts of daily life. When fathers embed values into rituals, they aren't just teaching, they're living the lessons they want their children to inherit.

These practices give values shape into something children can feel, remember, and eventually pass on. In this way, rituals do more than enrich the parenting journey. They become part of the legacy you leave behind: a living reflection of who you are, what you believe, and how you share your love.

## Building a ritual and tradition practice

For fathers looking to embed rituals and traditions into their parenting journey, the key is to start with intention, not the pursuit of perfection. Here are some guiding principles to help cultivate meaningful practices:

1. **Start small**: Rituals don't have to be elaborate to make an impact. Simple daily moments like a goodnight hug, a morning game, or reading a short book together, can become powerful anchors of connection over time.
2. **Be consistent**: Consistency helps rituals take root. Choose practices that naturally fit into your family's rhythm and protect them as sacred time. Even five minutes daily can become a cherished ritual.
3. **Involve your children**: Give your kids a voice in shaping family rituals. Whether choosing the Saturday breakfast menu or picking the bedtime story, their participation fosters

investment and joy.
4. **Celebrate milestones**: Use rituals to honour important transitions like birthdays, first days of school, lost teeth, or new achievements. These touchpoints reinforce values like growth, gratitude, and curiosity.
5. **Be flexible**: As children grow and family dynamics shift, rituals may need to evolve. What delights a toddler might feel outdated to a tween. Remaining adaptable keeps rituals relevant and emotionally resonant.

The most effective rituals aren't rigid, they respond to who your family is becoming. As life changes, so too will the form and meaning of your practices. This willingness to adapt not only keeps traditions alive, it strengthens your connection with your children through every age and stage.

Because in the end, rituals aren't just routines, they're intentional acts of love that build belonging, nurture identity, and leave behind a legacy that lasts far beyond childhood.

## The legacy of rituals

At their heart, rituals and traditions are about connection and care. They carve out space where fathers can be fully present, where children feel seen and valued, and where families come together to honour their shared journey. These practices transform the ordinary into the unforgettable, turning fleeting moments into lasting memories.

As fathers, the rituals we create and uphold become part of our legacy. They shape how our children understand love, navigate life's challenges, and build relationships of their own. They remind us that parenting isn't only defined by the major milestones but by the small, consistent acts that build trust, safety, and belonging.

Rituals are opportunities to lay a foundation of love, stability, and meaning. They're not about perfection or extravagance, they're about presence. And over time, these practices become the threads that weave generations together.

Rituals are like quiet gifts we leave behind. Our children may not yet understand their full significance, but one day when they repeat the same traditions with a child of their own, they'll realise how much those moments mattered.

# Reflective Questions

Take the time to reflect on these questions:

1. What are the small moments or rituals that your family looks forward to?
2. What traditions from your childhood would you like to revive—or reshape?
3. How can you use rituals to strengthen connection with your children?

# Communication is Key

*"Listening - really listening, is the hardest and most important part."*

Effective communication between parents is the foundation of a connected, compassionate, and collaborative family life. When parents communicate openly, respectfully, and thoughtfully, they cultivate a home grounded in trust, reducing tensions and strengthening emotional bonds.

Positive communication allows parents to function as a unified team, supporting each other and modelling cooperation for their children. It transforms parenting from a series of logistical decisions into a shared journey, where love and clarity guide the way.

Raising children is a shared responsibility and open dialogue is essential to maintaining balance, both at home and in the face of work and life pressures. When communication breaks down, it often gives way to frustration, resentment, or unspoken tension. But when parents regularly engage in honest conversations about their values, expectations, and evolving challenges, they create alignment and mutual understanding.

That alignment creates consistency for yourself, and your child. It provides a sense of safety, predictability, and shared purpose that children intuitively recognise and rely on.

In the end, effective communication doesn't just strengthen the partnership between parents, it provides children with a lived model of respect, empathy, and collaboration.

Parenting is challenging. It brings stress, fatigue, and inevitable moments of disagreement. But how parents manage these moments has a profound impact on the emotional wellbeing of the entire family.

When communication turns negative like arguing in front of children, using harsh tones, or shutting down emotionally, it introduces tension and uncertainty. In contrast, calm, respectful conversations, active listening, and collaborative problem-solving foster a positive, stable environment. These responses not only ease stress, they model what emotional maturity looks like in action. Which is often easier said than done.

One powerful tool for parents is the regular check-in. Taking intentional time to discuss personal concerns, family dynamics, and emotional wellbeing builds trust and mutual support. When parents feel emotionally held, they're better equipped to engage with their children from a place of calm and connection.

Children are always watching. They observe how conflict is handled, how love is expressed, how empathy is offered. These patterns quietly teach them how to express emotion, resolve disagreements, and engage in future relationships.

*"I'm scared that if I say the wrong thing, I'll shut them down forever."*

Maintaining open, respectful dialogue doesn't just preserve harmony, it gives children a sense of emotional safety. It teaches them that relationships can weather storms, that kindness matters, and that people, especially fathers) can lead with empathy and strength.

As a father, your example leaves a lasting imprint. It helps shape your child's expectations of what healthy relationships look and feel like and what to seek, offer, and protect as they grow.

## Establishing a shared vision

One of the first and most impactful steps in fostering effective communication between parents is creating a shared vision of what parenting looks like to both of you. This may begin before children arrive or may evolve over time as you grow into parenthood together. Either way, the process invites deep reflection, open dialogue, and, at times, outside perspective or guidance.

It means exploring and aligning on your individual and shared values, parenting styles, personal aspirations, and long-term hopes for your family across areas like finances, careers, lifestyle, family size, and the environment in which you hope to raise your child.

For example, as your child begins their learning journey, one parent might emphasise academic achievement, while the other prioritises emotional wellbeing or creative exploration. By discussing and aligning on these preferences early, parents can collaborate rather than compete, ensuring they're working toward a common purpose with mutual understanding.

Establishing a shared vision also means navigating conversations about roles, responsibilities, and expectations at home, at work, and within the emotional life of the family. These discussions may be unfamiliar or uncomfortable. You may not always know what your partner values most, or what they envision for the future. But engaging in these conversations with honesty and humility lays the groundwork for strong partnership and reduces the risk of future conflict.

A shared vision doesn't mean agreement on everything. It means committing to growing together, making space for each other's voices, and building a family life that reflects who you are, together.

These conversations often touch on very real, everyday dynamics like how household responsibilities are divided, how morning and bedtime routines are managed, or how each parent carves out time for themselves. You won't have all the answers figured out at once, and that's okay. What matters most is creating a relationship where these conversations can happen when they need to and with a foundation of curiosity, empathy, and mutual respect.

Taking a collaborative and open-minded approach doesn't just solve problems, it creates a culture of communication, where both parents feel seen, supported, and valued. It encourages honest dialogue without blame, and builds trust in one another's intentions.

The deeper purpose of establishing a shared parenting vision is to create a felt sense of "we're in this together." That foundation allows couples to navigate the inevitable challenges like the inevitable sleepless nights, conflicting priorities, and shifting goals with more grace and unity. It cultivates resilience, connection, and a shared understanding of what you're building together.

Because parenting isn't just about managing. It's about growing, as individuals and as a family. And that growth begins with being able to count on each other, communicate clearly, and create a home rooted in love and mutual commitment.

## Regular check-ins

Fatherhood is dynamic. As children grow and family circumstances shift, new challenges inevitably emerge. Regular check-ins between partners create space to pause, reassess, and adjust, ultimately ensuring that both parents remain connected, supported, and aligned.

These conversations can take many forms. They might be formal, like a weekly family meeting around the table, or informal which might be an honest chat on the couch after the kids are asleep. What matters most is consistency and care: creating a rhythm where reflection becomes a shared habit, not a crisis response.

---

*"Some of the best moments have come from simply sitting down and asking, 'How was your day?'"*

---

During these check-ins, the goal isn't always resolution. Sometimes, it's simply to listen fully and without interruption. Active listening is a powerful act: it communicates respect, empathy, and partnership. In holding space for each other's fears, hopes, and frustrations, couples deepen trust and strengthen their bond.

Over time, these check-ins become more than moments of communication. They become rituals of connection. A way to say: "I see you. I'm with you. We're in this together."

## Sharing responsibilities

Parenting is a team effort. Sharing responsibilities is essential for maintaining balance, preventing burnout, and fostering a healthy, respectful relationship. When one partner carries the bulk of the workload, whether in caregiving, household duties, or financial pressure, it can quietly erode connection and lead to feelings of resentment or imbalance. In contrast, sharing the weight creates a sense of partnership, mutual appreciation, and emotional safety.

Importantly, sharing responsibilities doesn't mean dividing everything equally, it means dividing them equitably. Each parent brings their own needs, capacities, and rhythms based on work commitments, personal energy, skills, and interests. Being a present and engaged parent means acknowledging these differences, not ignoring them.

When parents take time to establish a shared vision and openly discuss expectations, they're better equipped to navigate these complexities. This helps reduce unspoken assumptions, manage conflict with compassion, and reinforce the belief that both voices and contributions matter.

Ultimately, sharing responsibilities is not just about managing tasks, it's about living out your values. It's how love becomes action. And when children see that parenting is built on mutual respect, support, and flexibility, they absorb those values and carry them forward in their own relationships someday.

## Breaking down the mental load

The "mental load" refers to the invisible, often overlooked responsibilities involved in running a household and raising children. It includes everything from remembering appointments and managing school communications, to meal planning, keeping up with birthdays, packing essentials for outings, and anticipating needs before they arise.

In many homes, one partner, often the mother, carries the bulk of this ongoing mental labour. And because much of it is unseen, it's easy for its weight to be underestimated. Over time, this imbalance can lead to stress, emotional exhaustion, and feelings of resentment or isolation.

Addressing the mental load is more than just listing tasks and dividing them up. It's about revaluing roles that have historically been gendered or taken for granted. It's about recognising that caregiving is a form of leadership, and that managing the emotional rhythm of a family is just as vital as any financial or logistical task.

For fathers, this means stepping fully into the role of present, proactive partner, not as a "helper," but as an equal. It requires curiosity, humility, and a commitment to noticing what often goes unspoken. Rebalancing the mental load fosters deeper trust, reduces tension, and creates a more resilient family system. More than that, it models equity, empathy, and respect.

## Sharing the mental load

A critical first step in addressing the mental load is fostering open dialogue and a willingness to share responsibilities without minimising their significance. These tasks may seem small in isolation, but their cumulative weight can be overwhelming when carried by one person alone.

The mental load isn't just about the complexity or consequence of any single task. It's about the trust that a task, regardless how big or small, will be seen, remembered, and completed without prompting. That trust relieves the invisible burden of constant vigilance, planning, and emotional labour often carried by one partner.

Identifying the tasks that keep your household running, whether logistical, emotional, or relational, creates the foundation for real partnership. Once these tasks are made visible, they can be explicitly divided into shared responsibilities with clear ownership.

These responsibilities may include:

- Stocking the nappy bag before outings
- Taking the bins out
- Maintaining a running shopping list

- Paying bills and scheduling appointments
- Preparing meals and snacks
- Managing school communication
- Folding and putting away laundry

These are not just chores, they're acts of care that keep life functioning. While they often go unspoken, they are felt deeply when unacknowledged or left undone.

The goal is not perfection. It's about meaningful contribution. Sharing the mental load shows your partner you see them, value them, and are committed to building a household rooted in equity and trust.

The mental load is particularly pronounced in the early days of parenting, as new parents navigate steep learning curves, unpredictable routines, and shifting identities. With so much newness in the household like feedings, sleep schedules, emotional and physical recovery, it's easy for roles and expectations to become blurred or unspoken.

Open dialogue and clearly assigned responsibilities during this time can ease tension, reduce misunderstandings, and create a sense of shared ownership. The goal is not perfection but a steady movement toward balance, where both partners feel seen, supported, and valued in this new phase of life.

Importantly, the mental load isn't just logistical, it's also deeply emotional. Ensuring a newborn's safety, soothing a distressed baby, tracking developmental milestones, these tasks demand immense emotional energy. And when left to one partner alone, that load can become overwhelming.

Sharing these responsibilities fosters a stronger partnership, where both parents are actively engaged in the care and growth of their child.

It helps create a calmer, more connected home, where empathy not exhaustion, leads the way. And in doing so, parents model the kind of mutual respect and emotional presence they hope to pass on.

## Flexibility and adaptability

Finding balance across work, parenting, and personal life is rarely a perfect equation. That's why flexibility is essential, not just as a practical tool, but as a mindset for navigating the unpredictable nature of raising a family while managing professional demands.

Flexibility takes many forms. It begins with mutual understanding and active negotiation. For instance, if one partner faces an unusually demanding week at work, the other may need to temporarily take on more responsibilities at home. These moments require a spirit of collaboration, not rigid expectations but an understanding that roles will ebb and flow, while the commitment to support remains constant.

Adaptability also becomes increasingly important as children grow. Their needs, routines, and emotional landscapes evolve, sometimes rapidly. Parents who stay open to renegotiating roles and expectations are better equipped to meet these shifts with patience and grace.

It's not about splitting everything evenly. It's about showing up with empathy and being willing to reassess and realign as life changes. That's how families stay connected, resilient, and rooted in shared purpose even when the winds shift.

## Building a culture of appreciation

A strong parenting partnership thrives on mutual appreciation. Amid the physical and emotional demands of raising children, it's easy to overlook each other's efforts or assume they're understood without being spoken. But small, consistent expressions of gratitude through words, gestures, or quiet acts of kindness have a lasting impact. They reinforce connection, ease stress, and breathe energy into the partnership.

Fostering a culture of appreciation also models powerful behaviours for children. When they see parents thanking one another, offering encouragement, or acknowledging effort, they learn that care is reciprocal, and contribution is valued. This, in turn, encourages children to take initiative, express gratitude, and participate in the household as active, engaged members.

Acknowledging your partner's contributions no matter how routine, strengthens a sense of teamwork and validation. Thanking your child for helping with dinner, showing up with a kind word after a long day, or simply noticing when someone tries, that's where the emotional glue of family is strengthened.

Appreciation doesn't require grand gestures. A quiet "thank you," an unexpected hug, or taking over a task so someone else can rest can speak volumes. These moments, repeated over time, help build a home where kindness flows freely and connection runs deep.

## Celebrating wins together

Parenting is full of milestones, both monumental and modest. Whether it's a baby's first steps, mastering toilet training, or reaching a goal at school, celebrating these wins as a family strengthens connection, pride, and a shared sense of purpose.

These moments are more than occasions for applause, they're opportunities to pause, reflect, and take pride in the partnership behind the parenting. Each milestone represents not only your child's growth, but your shared effort in building a loving, supportive family.

Celebrating wins also sends two powerful messages to your child:

- **"You did it."** It affirms that when they work toward something with focus, effort, and persistence they're capable of achieving it.
- **"We see you."** It reinforces that their efforts are acknowledged, valued, and supported, and you are paying attention and cheering them on.

These celebrations don't need to be extravagant. What matters is the presence, the recognition, and the emotion behind it. In time, these small moments of joy will become big memories that are woven into your family's narrative of resilience, encouragement, and love.

## Navigating conflict

Conflict and tension are natural parts of life and parenting is no exception. In fact, even minor disagreements can feel magnified under the weight of exhaustion, time pressure, and the constant demands of raising children. When personal time is scarce and stress is high, it's easy for unresolved tensions to linger.

*"When I stopped trying to 'fix' everything and just listened, our whole family shifted."*

Disagreements may arise around discipline, finances, household responsibilities, or simply differences in parenting philosophy. How couples respond to these conflicts has a profound impact, not only on the health of the relationship, but on the emotional climate of the home and the example set for their children.

Empathy is one of the most powerful tools available in these moments. By pausing to see the situation through your partner's eyes and validating how they feel, you create an environment where both voices matter. This sense of mutual understanding opens the door to more constructive, calm conversations.

With compassion at the centre, couples are better able to identify root causes, navigate differences, and collaborate on meaningful solutions. Empathy doesn't eliminate conflict but it transforms the way conflict is experienced, making space for connection, growth, and healing even in the hardest moments.

## Staying solution-oriented

When conflict arises, it's easy to slip into blame or defensiveness but real progress begins with a shared focus on solutions. Taking a solution-oriented approach helps couples shift from opposition to collaboration, especially during stressful parenting moments.

This process starts with identifying the real issue—not just the surface disagreement, but the needs, stressors, or expectations underlying it. Together, partners can define the problem, explore contributing factors, and co-create a way forward.

Effective problem-solving includes:

- Pausing to reflect on what's really happening beneath the tension
- Brainstorming ideas together, without judgment or rushing
- Discussing potential approaches, then weighing impact and feasibility
- Agreeing on a plan that feels fair, supportive, and flexible

It's important not to jump straight into "fixing." Slowing down to name the issue and work as a team builds trust and prevents repeat friction.

Once a solution is agreed upon, put it into action with an open mind. Stay flexible. If the approach doesn't work, treat it not as a failure but as feedback, an opportunity to adapt and try again. What matters most is working together, staying curious, and keeping your connection intact through it all.

## Building a support network

A strong support network extends far beyond the walls of your home. Friends, family, and community resources all play a vital role in easing the pressures of parenting and helping families thrive. Coordinating playdates or connecting with other parents not only gives children valuable social opportunities, it also offers parents a chance to share stories, strategies, and solidarity.

Parenting is profoundly rewarding, but it's also demanding. There is no shame in seeking support. Whether it's asking grandparents for help, hiring a babysitter to recharge, or joining a local parenting group, these resources offer perspective, connection, and relief.

Sometimes, support looks like turning to others in a different way. Couples may benefit from professional guidance whether through therapy, counselling, or parenting workshops. A neutral third party can offer fresh insights, communication tools, and space to reflect without blame. Seeking help in this way isn't a sign of strain, it's a sign of strength. A proactive step that affirms your commitment to growth, partnership, and the wellbeing of your family.

No one is meant to do this alone. Leaning on a support network either formal or informal, isn't just helpful, it's healthy, wise and ultimately, sustainable.

## Positive communication

Investing in communication yields deep and lasting benefits for both parents and children. A strong foundation of open, respectful dialogue fosters a home that feels stable, nurturing, and emotionally safe, where children grow up feeling secure and loved.

Positive communication also models healthy relationship dynamics. It teaches children through observation and experience, the importance of teamwork, empathy, mutual respect, and emotional literacy. These lessons stay with them, influencing how they build relationships of their own.

*"Learning to listen, to really listen has deepened the love in our family."*

For parents, strong communication reinforces the partnership itself. It creates space for appreciation, personal growth, and shared resilience. It allows couples to meet challenges not in isolation, but together with greater confidence, compassion, and joy.

This collaborative approach doesn't just strengthen the bond between partners, it enhances the wellbeing of the entire family. It builds a culture of trust and support, where everyone feels heard, valued, and deeply connected.

## Strengthening communication

To build and maintain a strong model for positive communication, you may consider these practical, compassionate approaches:

1. **Schedule regular check-ins**: Set aside consistent time to talk about parenting goals, household responsibilities, and any concerns. These moments help prevent small frustrations from

becoming larger tensions.
2. **Use "I" statements**: When discussing sensitive topics, frame your thoughts using "I" language e.g., "I feel overwhelmed when I don't have time to exercise" to express needs without triggering defensiveness.
3. **Express gratitude daily**: Thank your partner for their efforts, no matter how big or small. Acknowledgement reinforces the emotional bond and creates a more appreciative home atmosphere.
4. **Seek guidance when needed**: If conversations become difficult or repetitive conflicts arise, consider therapy or professional support. It's a powerful sign of commitment, not weakness.
5. **Celebrate milestones**: Honour parenting, personal, and developmental achievements. Acknowledging wins reinforces partnership and adds joy to the shared journey.
6. **Divide and conquer**: Use shared tools like calendars or task apps to clarify and distribute responsibilities. Transparency reduces stress and ensures equity in managing family life.
7. **Prioritise quality time**: In the chaos of parenting, make space for each other. A regular date night or a quiet evening at home helps maintain connection and intimacy.

Positive communication is foundational to navigating the complex dance between work, life, and parenting. When couples foster open dialogue, divide responsibilities with care, and show up with mutual respect, they create a home that doesn't just function, it thrives.

This investment in your relationship models something powerful for children. It says that love grows through listening, that conflict can be met with grace, and that relationships rooted in kindness and shared purpose build resilience across a lifetime.

## Reflective Questions

Take the time to reflect on these questions:

1. How would you rate your communication with your partner and children?
2. What makes you feel heard and respected and do you offer that to others?
3. What's one conversation you've been avoiding that might bring your family closer?

# Building Resilience

*"I've had to rebuild myself more than once. That's part of the journey – falling and standing again."*

Fatherhood is a profound and transformative journey but it also comes with its share of challenges. From sleepless nights with a newborn baby to navigating household tension, shifting identities, and bouts of self-doubt, the path is rarely straightforward.

Balancing the unpredictability of raising children, nurturing a connected relationship, and staying present and effective at work can test even the most prepared parent. In these moments, resilience, which is often defined as the capacity to adapt, recover, and grow through adversity, becomes a vital skill and a guiding force.

Resilience isn't about avoiding hardship. It's about engaging with it, and ultimately developing healthy coping strategies, practicing self-care, and maintaining a mindset grounded in possibility and self-compassion. It's the ability to bend without breaking, to learn from the struggle, and to rise with deeper clarity and strength.

For fathers, cultivating resilience is not only essential for personal wellbeing, it is a quiet form of leadership. Your response to stress, setbacks, and uncertainty becomes a living lesson for your child in how to face life with courage, optimism, and grace.

Because how you show up, through the mess, during the hard days, and in the early mornings, it all models for your child what it means to stay grounded when things feel uncertain. And that, more than anything, is a legacy worth passing on.

## Understanding resilience in fatherhood

Resilience in fatherhood isn't about avoiding difficulty. It's about equipping yourself with the tools and mindset to meet challenges head-on. It means developing skills like emotional regulation, adaptability, and problem-solving. In practice, that may look like staying calm during a tantrum, juggling competing demands, or maintaining a sense of humour and teamwork in the midst of daily chaos at home and at work.

A key part of resilience is accepting that struggle is normal. Many parents fall into the trap of believing they should have everything under control. But that unrealistic expectation only leads to self-doubt, guilt, and burnout when things (inevitably) don't go according to plan.

This pressure extends into every area of life: the tug-of-war between work and home, the slow erosion of time with friends, and the challenge of making space for yourself and your partner. These are common tensions not personal failings.

Resilience asks something different. It invites you to embrace imperfection. To acknowledge your limits without shame. And to see each obstacle not as a setback but as an invitation to grow stronger, more intentional, and more compassionate.

## Recognising and managing stress

The first step in managing stress is simply recognising it. Everyone experiences stress differently, and your ability to cope, recognise your triggers, and how you react may look entirely different from those around you. But certain signs are common: irritability, difficulty concentrating, disrupted sleep, feeling overwhelmed, or physical symptoms like headaches and fatigue.

Your personal stress response is shaped by your upbringing, life experiences, natural coping habits, and the support systems you have around you. Still, there are common categories of stress that impact physical, emotional, and mental wellbeing:

- **Emotional stress**: Feelings of guilt, worry, frustration, or being constantly overwhelmed
- **Financial stress**: Concerns about income, bills, affording essentials, and feeling pressure to provide
- **Social stress**: Fears of growing distant from friends, not meeting societal parenting expectations, or feeling isolated

Whatever the source of your stress, it can drain your energy and presence, making it harder to be the parent, partner, and person you want to be. If stress is left unaddressed, it can lead to emotional burnout and ripple through your relationships, your focus and effectiveness.

---

*"I've been through hard times before—but being a father hits differently. The stakes are higher."*

---

While managing stress begins with awareness, it continues through proactive care. That might mean setting boundaries, asking for help, creating space for rest, or simply naming what's hard.

Addressing stress isn't a detour from parenting. It's part of it. Because the more you tend to your wellbeing, the more fully you can show up for yourself, your partner, and your child.

## Creating a supportive environment

A supportive environment is essential for managing stress and building lasting resilience. This includes both the physical space you inhabit and the emotional ecosystem you cultivate around you.

Some days it may feel impossible, but at home, creating or maintaining a tidy and organised environment can reduce daily friction and provide a sense of calm amidst the unpredictability of parenting. Small changes like decluttering high-traffic areas or creating dedicated spaces for rest and play can have a big impact on daily mood and mental clarity.

Just as important is your emotional support network. Sharing responsibilities with your partner, asking for help from family members, joining a parenting group or establishing a wisdom collective, can ease the pressure and offer new perspectives. These connections don't just lighten the load; they remind you that you're not alone.

Being proactive about support is not a sign of weakness, it's an investment in your wellbeing and in your ability to show up with presence, patience, and love.

Creating a strong support system allows you to meet challenges with steadiness and self-compassion, and that's the kind of strength that truly supports your family.

## Prioritising physical and mental health

Parenting often calls for selflessness, regularly putting your child's needs first. While this instinct is admirable, neglecting your own wellbeing can quietly erode your ability to show up with patience, energy, and care over the long-term. Burnout doesn't announce itself loudly. It builds, slowly, in the moments when rest is skipped and needs go unspoken.

Prioritising your physical and mental health is not selfish, which can be the initial reaction. However, it's essential for sustaining resilience. It allows you to meet each new season of parenting with steadiness and strength. Whether it's a toddler learning to walk, a child seeking support with big emotions, or a teen needing presence and perspective, your health is the foundation for that connection long into the future.

This isn't just about surviving the early years. It's about preparing for the long haul, being the kind of father who's active, engaged, and emotionally available as your child continues to grow. It means recognising that your wellbeing matters because theirs does too.

Tending to your health, through rest, movement, reflection, friendship, or simply stepping outside for air, isn't a break from parenting. It's a vital part of it.

## Embracing the unpredictability

Parenting is inherently unpredictable. Just when it feels like a rhythm has been found, a growth spurt, illness, or developmental leap can disrupt the flow, leaving you feeling like you're starting all over again.

Resilience in fatherhood isn't just about managing stress, it's about meeting change with flexibility, humour, and good grace. It is recognising that unpredictability doesn't reflect your level of competence, it's simply comes with the territory.

Adapting to change means letting go of perfection and anchoring yourself in presence. It means understanding that routines are helpful but not unbreakable. And it means giving yourself the permission to pivot, to reset, and to try again.

Change is not a verdict on your ability. It's an invitation to grow alongside your child, to meet each moment with compassion for them, and for yourself.

## Reframing challenges as opportunities

Reframing challenges as opportunities for growth helps fathers approach parenting's inevitable difficulties with greater grace and presence. It doesn't require pretending that hard moments aren't hard, but it invites a more generous way of interpreting them.

For example, a toddler's defiance can feel deeply frustrating for any parent, but it may also be understood as a necessary expression of independence and development. A sleepless night may leave you exhausted but it can also become an unexpected window for quiet connection, whether through gentle rocking or simply being there so your partner can rest.

*"Resilience isn't about being tough—it's about staying open even when things are hard."*

Reframing isn't about dismissing discomfort. It's about creating space for empathy toward your child, your partner, and yourself. It's choosing to see challenge as part of the learning curve, rather than as a measure of failure.

Over time, this mindset builds emotional flexibility. It helps fathers stay grounded in moments of chaos, and turn struggle into something meaningful like a moment of connection, a lesson in patience, or a new kind of resilience.

## Letting go of control

For many parents, the instinct to plan and control every detail of family life is strong. From bedtime routines, screen time limits, where they sleep, and when they eat. But the truth is, so much of parenting unfolds beyond our control. Children grow, moods shift, routines break, and plans unravel. It is all part of life as a parent.

Learning to embrace this unpredictability can be quietly liberating. It invites self-compassion in place of self-judgment. It allows space for curiosity instead of frustration. And it offers the reminder that not everything needs to be fixed, only met with presence.

By focusing on what can be controlled, including your own mindset, reactions, and ability to return to calm, you create steadiness, even when circumstances change. While it may feel counter intuitive, letting go becomes a strength, not a surrender.

There will always be another bedtime, another conversation, another chance. And sometimes, the gentlest way to lead your child is to show them how to breathe through change, and approach disruption with grace.

## Humour helps

Laughter is one of the most powerful tools for resilience. It doesn't erase the challenges, but it makes them feel a little lighter, a little more human. Whether it's finding humour in a chaotic nappy explosion, sharing a parenting mishap with a mate, or sending a perfectly timed meme to your partner, these moments matter. They create release, restore perspective, and build connection.

Parenting is serious business, but it's also wildly funny. Toddlers with big opinions, snack negotiations, unexpected messes, and bedtime stand-offs often come with a side of absurdity. Taking a moment to laugh at the situation, at yourself, or with your partner, can shift the energy and reframe the moment.

Reflecting on and sharing these moments doesn't just help you move past the tough parts, it anchors you in the joy. It reminds you that alongside the responsibility and emotional labour, there is fun, spontaneity, and lightness to be found.

Because when you laugh together, you remember you're not just surviving parenthood. You're living it fully, imperfectly, and often hilariously.

## Cultivating connections

Building and maintaining meaningful connections takes effort, but that effort is deeply worthwhile. Whether it's hosting playdates, joining a parenting group, attending a workshop, or simply walking with a friend, these moments create space to share stories, gain new perspectives, and have conversations that aren't solely about parenting.

Staying connected with others helps anchor your identity in something broader than your role as a parent. It offers relief from the isolation that can creep in during the early months, when sleep is scarce, emotions are high, and the days feel all-consuming.

Even a simple practice like a weekly coffee with a friend or a regular chat with another parent, can become a lifeline. These rituals offer laughter, validation, and perspective, reminding you that you're not alone, and that this journey, while intense, is also shared.

Connection is not a luxury. It is part of the scaffolding that supports resilience, restores energy, and reminds you that you matter, too.

## Building resilience in children

While parents benefit from developing resilience themselves, one of their most powerful roles is passing it on. Children learn how to navigate life's challenges not just through instruction, but through observation. They knowingly and unknowingly watch and take in how you handle stress, recover from setbacks, and move forward with hope, optimism and also caution.

By modelling healthy coping strategies and a constructive mindset, parents lay the foundation for children to build their own resilience. This might mean staying calm in difficult moments, finding solutions collaboratively, or approaching challenges with patience and perspective.

When a child faces adversity, whether at home, at school, or in the playground, encouraging them to reflect and brainstorm solutions, rather than rushing in to fix the problem, helps build confidence. It teaches them that they have agency, that their voice matters, and that they're capable of overcoming obstacles.

Equally important is emotional validation. Whether it's frustration with a puzzle, sadness over a lost toy, or disappointment when things don't go their way, acknowledging those feelings teaches children that emotions are not to be feared or suppressed. They are part of the human experience. And learning to feel, name and move through them is a cornerstone of resilience and ability to better manage relationships.

Through encouragement, modelling, and a commitment to connection, you offer your child an extraordinary gift: the belief that no matter what life throws their way, they can adapt, grow, and meet it with courage.

## Celebrating effort, not just outcomes

Praising effort, rather than focusing solely on outcomes, reinforces the value of perseverance, growth, and the courage to keep trying. When we acknowledge a child's hard work on a drawing, even if it isn't "perfect," we're sending a powerful message: your effort matters. This encourages children to take pride in the process, not just the result.

Recognising effort also creates space for ongoing development, whether in art, writing, sport, or the small daily acts of problem-solving and persistence. It helps children understand that improvement comes through consistency, curiosity, and trying again.

These are teachable moments in resilience. Celebrating effort teaches that:

- Growth happens in the process
- Failure isn't something to avoid. It is something to learn from
- Support is something you can ask for and offer
- Success isn't just about achievement; it's also about the journey that led there

By focusing on the "how" just as much as the "what," parents help children internalise a growth mindset. One that says: your value doesn't depend on perfection, but on the way you show up, try again, and keep going.

That's the kind of celebration that lasts.

## The long-term benefits of resilience

Cultivating resilience yields lasting benefits for both parents and children. Resilient parents are better equipped to weather the highs and lows of family life, enabling them to navigate the uncertainty, stress, and emotional demands of parenting with greater calm and presence. This emotional steadiness creates a home environment that is stable, nurturing, and secure.

In turn, this kind of environment fosters secure attachment and emotional wellbeing in children. It teaches them, through lived experience, that while life is unpredictable, they are safe, supported, and capable.

For children, growing up in a resilience-focused household becomes a blueprint for future strength. They learn how to navigate setbacks, adapt to change, and face challenges with curiosity and confidence. They internalise the message: "you don't have to be perfect to be strong. You just have to keep showing up."

By modelling and teaching resilience, parents give their children something far more enduring than momentary success. They offer them tools to navigate the world with grit, empathy, and grace; a lifelong gift that will shape how they relate to themselves, to others, and to the world around them.

## Practical strategies for building resilience

Fatherhood brings with it natural highs and lows and having intentional strategies for building resilience can help you navigate both with greater clarity, calm, and connection.

Here are some grounding practices that support your wellbeing along the way:

1. **Practice mindfulness**: Techniques like deep breathing, meditation, or short grounding exercises help anchor you in the present and reduce emotional reactivity in stressful moments.
2. **Cultivate self-compassion**: Talk to yourself with the same

kindness you'd offer a close friend. Acknowledge that parenting is hard and that bad days don't define you.
3. **Establish steady routines**: Predictable rhythms offer a sense of control and stability, even when the wider world feels chaotic. Routines can become a source of comfort for both you and your child.
4. **Keep the bigger picture in view**: In the thick of a tough moment, zoom out. Remind yourself that tantrums end, growth takes time, and most storms do pass.
5. **Stay connected**: Reach out to friends, family, or parenting communities. Sharing experiences reduces isolation and brings in fresh perspective and warmth.
6. **Celebrate small wins**: Acknowledge moments of effort, progress, or survival. These small recognitions build momentum and reinforce that you're doing better than you think.
7. **Set realistic expectations**: Let go of perfection. Aim instead for presence, patience, and progress. These qualities build strength, not pressure.
8. **Seek support when needed**: Whether it's a partner, a friend, or a mental health professional, talking things through can ease the load and offer clarity when it feels hard to find your footing.

Parenthood is a journey woven with challenges, setbacks, and profound joy. By cultivating a practice of resilience, you equip yourself with the tools, relationships, and mindset needed to navigate its twists and turns with purpose and grace.

---

*"Fatherhood gives me strength I didn't know I had. Their love pulls me through."*

Managing stress, prioritising your health, and embracing unpredictability isn't just good practice, it's a gift. One that creates a strong, sustainable foundation for both you and your family.

Resilience empowers you not just to survive, but to thrive. And in doing so, you offer your child one of life's most powerful lessons: that they too can face uncertainty and adversity with courage, adaptability, and hope.

With the right mindset, meaningful support, and practical strategies, you can transform obstacles into opportunities for growth. You can turn everyday moments into learning experiences. And you can build a family life that is both grounded and joyful, one where strength is quiet, effort is celebrated, and love is the throughline.

# Reflective Questions

Take the time to reflect on these questions:

1. What's one tough moment in fatherhood you've made it through and what did it teach you?
2. How do you currently care for your own emotional resilience?
3. Who or what helps you keep going when things feel overwhelming?

# Energy and Focus

*"Feeling fit and strong is important for me if I am to feel capable and confident. It also enables me to be a better father."*

Fatherhood is deeply rewarding but also undeniably demanding. It often requires a delicate balance between professional responsibilities, family commitments, and personal aspirations. For many fathers, maintaining physical health, mental clarity, and emotional resilience becomes essential to staying grounded and present, both at home and at work.

And yet, these core pillars of wellbeing which include exercise, sleep, and focus, are often the first to be sacrificed in the whirlwind of daily life. When the desire to be engaged, available, and effective stretches across every domain, something inevitably gives. The tension is subtle but persistent with the internal debate between what your family needs and what you personally value and require to feel whole.

This tug-of-war can surface as guilt, wondering whether time spent on personal needs might be perceived as selfish, or do you quietly choose to let go of things that once brought energy or joy, like exercise, gaming, reading, or creative pursuits. Over time, these small trade-offs accumulate, often unnoticed, eroding vitality and increasing emotional fatigue.

But effective and sustainable fatherhood isn't about erasing the self. It's about integration, where you find rhythms, rituals, and support systems that allow your identity to include (not exclude) the parts of you that fuel growth and joy.

## Exercise and its afterglow

Exercise is a cornerstone of health, with lasting benefits that reach far beyond physical fitness. For fathers, staying active isn't just about appearance or performance, it's about sustaining the energy, clarity, and stamina needed to meet the daily demands of parenting, work, and life with presence and focus.

And yet, exercise is often the first thing to slip away. In the early weeks of fatherhood, carving out time for a run or a gym session can feel selfish or unfair to your partner. But this isn't just time "for you." It's time that strengthens your capacity to show up, long-term, in all the roles you care most about. Obviously in the early days, this requires communication, negotiation, and recognising your partners needs.

Feeling strong, confident, and grounded in your body has a ripple effect, it supports sharper focus at work, more patience at home, and greater emotional bandwidth. It helps you keep pace with your growing child, both physically and emotionally.

The reality is that you only get one body and keeping it healthy, mobile, and strong is a profound investment for your future. This investment is not just in yourself, but in the quality of time you'll share with your family. Building a sustainable exercise routine, even in small ways, lays the foundation for a future filled with adventure, vitality, and connection

## Boosting energy levels

One of the most immediate benefits of regular exercise is a noticeable lift in energy. Aerobic activities like running, swimming, or cycling improve cardiovascular health, helping the body deliver oxygen and nutrients for more efficiently fuelling both body and mind.

Endurance exercises can also offer a kind of mental clarity. For some, they create space to focus, decompress, or simply be present. For others, they spark imagination, prompting reflection, idea generation, or problem-solving. These moments of internal movement are as valuable as the physical ones.

Strength training brings a different kind of focus. It builds muscle, enhances functional capacity, and requires intentional awareness of form, breath, and technique. Reframing weight training as a practice of functional strength to be physically capable father rather than just aesthetics, can help shift your motivation. It becomes less about the mirror, and more about sustaining long-term vitality and mobility for fatherhood to play, wrestle and even hold your child with ease as they grow.

Even short bursts of movement can ripple outward. A 30-minute session in the morning or at lunch might leave you sharper at work, calmer at home, and more present with your family in the evening. These are not "extra" moments, they're essential ones.

Because when you move your body, you're not just building endurance. You're replenishing the energy that fuels patience, joy, and meaningful connection.

## Mental health and movement

Exercise is one of the most powerful tools for supporting mental health. Physical activity triggers the release of endorphins, which are the "feel-good" hormones that help reduce stress, ease anxiety, and lift mood. For fathers navigating the constant demands of work, family, and personal growth, this emotional lift can be a vital reset.

Beyond the chemical benefits, movement offers something subtler: mental space. A solo run, a stretch of quiet yoga, a game of basketball with friends, these aren't just physical outlets. They're moments of reconnection, where the noise recedes and clarity returns.

Prioritising exercise doesn't mean chasing performance, it means creating space to feel centred, capable, and present. Fathers who build in regular movement often report being better equipped to meet the emotional and logistical challenges of parenting, and more available to themselves, their partners, and their children.

Because when you move your body with intention, you make space for your mind to settle, your mood to lift, and your resilience to expand.

## Setting a positive example

Beyond personal wellbeing, exercise offers fathers a powerful opportunity to model healthy habits for their children. When kids see their dad prioritising movement, whether it's structured or spontaneous, they internalise a message that physical activity is valuable, normal, and even joyful.

It's important to remember that "exercise" isn't confined to the gym. It can look like hiking on the weekend, surfing at sunrise, playing park footy, or climbing trees together. It's anything that gets your body moving, sparks curiosity or skill-building, and connects you with the world beyond your front door.

While it might not always be realistic to include your family in every activity, creating an active family culture offers lasting benefits:

- You model consistency and care for health
- You create moments of connection and shared memory
- You cultivate motivation, together
- You embed movement into your child's world as something relational, not just routine

In the long run, these experiences don't just support physical health, they deepen trust, build traditions, and show your child that strength and closeness can grow side by side.

## The impacts of sleep depravation

Sleep is increasingly recognised as a pillar of overall wellbeing, but it often remains overlooked in the scramble to balance work, life, and family. For parents, adequate rest isn't a luxury. It's a necessity. Yet it's often the first thing to go, especially in the demanding early years of raising children.

Sleep deprivation can take a serious toll. It affects physical health, emotional regulation, decision-making, and your ability to show up meaningfully at work and at home. Without rest, stress escalates. Irritability rises. Patience wanes. And it becomes harder to offer the calm, present support your child or partner may need most.

Chronic sleep disruption compounds this strain. It can contribute to anxiety, depression, weakened immunity, migraines, and other stress-related symptoms. Perhaps most quietly, it dulls joy. Ultimately, making it harder to laugh, engage, or connect in the ways that matter most.

Sleep isn't just about recovery, it's about resourcefulness. It sharpens focus, strengthens memory, and bolsters your ability to solve problems creatively and calmly. Parents who are consistently sleep-deprived often find themselves struggling to be both productive at work and fully present at home.

Prioritising sleep is not self-indulgent. It's foundational. It's what allows both parents to access the emotional resilience needed to sustain loving relationships, handle challenges with grace, and build a home where everyone feels safe, seen, and supported.

## Prioritising quality over quantity

As a father, there's no shortage of commentary about how little sleep you're getting or how much you wish you had. While it's well known that adults need 7–9 hours of sleep each night, this often isn't realistic during the early months of parenthood. And yet, quality can be just as important as quantity when it comes to rest and recovery.

The conversation around sleep is often a silent tension point in the household, especially in those early, blurry weeks. It's important to acknowledge that mothers frequently bear the brunt of sleep disruption, due to feeding schedules, unsettled sleep patterns, and the physical recovery from birth. This imbalance is not just logistical, it's emotional too.

For fathers, this presents a moment of choice. A chance to reflect on "how" and "where" they can show up to support their partner and rebalance the load. Whether it's handling the next feed, offering a morning sleep-in, or simply being attuned to the silent cues of exhaustion, these small choices become acts of partnership.

In this season, sleep may be broken or brief. But what matters most is the shared effort, the compassion in the cracks, and the commitment to care—for each other, and for yourselves.

## Finding better sleep

Sleep quality and quantity will naturally fluctuate, especially in the early months of parenting. But even when uninterrupted rest feels out of reach, there are meaningful ways to create an environment that supports deeper, more restorative sleep for both you and your partner.

Consider the following strategies:

- **Set shared expectations**: Have clear conversations about

night-time responsibilities. Whether it's sharing feeds, taking turns with early mornings, or settling an unsettled baby, setting expectations helps reduce tension and foster teamwork.
- **Establish a consistent routine**: Going to bed at the same time each night helps regulate your body's internal clock. A calming routine with baths, books, and low light signals to your mind and body to wind down, and builds rituals that comfort the whole family.
- **Create a sleep-friendly environment**: Use soft lighting, install blackout curtains, minimise outside noise, and regulate the room's temperature to create a calming, cocoon-like space. Consider using humidifiers or white noise machines to enhance comfort.
- **Limit screen time before bed**: Reducing exposure to screens in the hour before sleep helps protect your natural sleep-wake cycle. Setting boundaries around device use can also prevent late-night "doom scrolling," a common habit when exhaustion meets idle time, especially while feeding or soothing a child.

## The power of focus in balancing priorities

Focus is not a static trait, it's an evolving practice. At its core, focus is the ability to direct your attention and energy with intention, whether toward a goal, a task, or a moment of connection. But in reality, this is often easier said than done.

For many fathers, the desire to be present and engaged at home constantly competes with the demands of work, the pull of friendships, and the need for personal time and space. Focus becomes a balancing act, that is less about perfection and more about navigating shifting priorities with clarity and self-compassion.

Balancing work, family, and personal aspirations requires more than just time management. It calls for value alignment, which can be the willingness to ask, again and again: "What matters most right now?"

By noticing where your attention drifts, where your energy is replenished, and where it's drained, you can begin to shape a rhythm that honours both your commitments and your deeper values.

Because presence isn't just about proximity. It's about attention. And when you learn to direct your focus toward what matters most, you don't just survive the juggle, you start to shape a life that feels aligned, intentional, and whole.

## Avoid multitasking

It's easy to fall into the belief that juggling multiple responsibilities at once is the key to getting everything done. But the myth of multitasking often leads to diminished focus, reduced efficiency, and heightened stress. Research shows that switching between tasks actually taxes the brain, leading to slower progress and more mistakes.

For fathers balancing family, work, and personal goals, trying to be everywhere at once can leave you feeling scattered and depleted. Instead, focusing on one task at a time allows for greater attention to detail, deeper connection, and a more grounded sense of completion.

This might mean time-blocking a focused window to engage fully with your child or carving out a defined space to tackle a project. By keeping the activity time-bound, you create clear start and finish lines, allowing your attention to be both present and purposeful.

Single-tasking isn't about doing less. It's about doing what matters well and giving yourself permission to bring your full self to one moment at a time.

## Setting boundaries

Establishing clear boundaries between work and family life is essential to maintaining focus and emotional balance. Fathers who intentionally set aside time for work, family, and self-care often find it easier to manage their responsibilities without becoming overwhelmed or consumed by guilt when one area spills into another.

Boundaries are not about restriction; they're about clarity. They allow you to show up fully in each role, knowing there's space carved out for what matters.

But setting boundaries is only half the work. Sustaining them requires conscious communication with your partner, your colleagues, and anyone else who may place demands on your time, energy, or attention. By naming your limits and expressing your intentions, you create shared understanding and reduce the mental load of constantly renegotiating your availability.

These conversations might feel awkward at first, but they create room for deeper connection, mutual support, and emotional sustainability.

Boundaries aren't barriers. They're the quiet scaffolding that helps you honour your values, protect your energy, and stay connected to what matters most.

## Practicing mindfulness

Mindfulness is a powerful and accessible tool for strengthening focus and reducing stress. For fathers navigating competing demands, whether at work or at home, it offers a way to stay grounded, steady, and present.

Practicing mindfulness doesn't require long stretches of silence or perfect stillness. It can be as simple as pausing to notice your breath, tuning into your body, or observing the moment without judgment. These small pauses can create space between stimulus and response, allowing clarity and composure to return.

Techniques might include:

- **Deep breathing**: A few intentional breaths can reset your nervous system, especially in emotionally charged moments.
- **Short meditations**: Just 5–10 minutes of guided stillness can reduce mental clutter and restore balance.
- **Reflective pauses**: Whether you're washing the dishes, in the car, or beside your child's bed, taking a moment to check in with your body and thoughts can shift your entire internal landscape.

By building mindfulness into your daily rhythm, you cultivate not just attention, but intention, choosing how to respond, rather than react. Over time, it becomes less about finding calm and more about returning to it... Again and again.

## Exercise, sleep, and focus

Fatherhood is a journey of growth, unpredictability, and emotional depth. It asks you to manage stress, embrace the highs and lows, and navigate moments of doubt, all while nurturing your child and strengthening your relationship. Amid this complexity, caring for your own wellbeing isn't optional, it is absolutely essential.

You may already recognise the importance of exercise, sleep, and focused attention. But integrating these pillars into a full and demanding life can feel daunting. Here's how to bring them into rhythm with your reality:

- **Anchor small habits**: Start with realistic micro-practices: a

15-minute walk before breakfast, five mindful breaths before meetings, or lights-out 30 minutes earlier three nights a week. Consistency beats intensity.
- **Build "wellbeing windows"**: Identify natural breaks in your day like school drop-offs, nap times, lunch hours, and use those as gentle pockets of time to reset, move, or rest.
- **Integrate, don't add**: Combine quality time with movement (bike rides, backyard soccer), reflection with routine (mindful washing dishes or in the shower), and focus with connection (leaving your phone in another room during story time).
- **Co-create supportive routines**: Collaborate with your partner to design weekly rhythms that honour both your needs. Shared calendars, alternate self-care nights, or child-free "recharge windows" can make a big difference.
- **Accept the ebbs and flows**: Some weeks will be messier than others and that's okay. Integration is about returning to what matters when life wobbles, not punishing yourself when it does.

By weaving wellbeing into your daily landscape, you reinforce the foundation of your fatherhood. Not as a perfect balance—but as a living practice that grows with you.

## Making time for exercise

The transition to fatherhood can be a profound shift—suddenly, your time is no longer solely your own. You're pulled between roles, responsibilities, and a desire to be present in each of them. In this context, making time and finding motivation for exercise becomes not just important but deeply personal.

Here are three ways to keep movement part of your world:

1. **Start small**: Even 10–15 minutes of activity a day can make a difference. A walk around the block, a quick home workout, or a lunchtime jog counts. Something is always better than nothing.
2. **Combine exercise with family time**: Choose activities like bike rides, hikes, or park play that allow you to move your body and connect with your child at the same time. These moments build memories and muscle.
3. **Schedule it like it matters (because it does)**: Block time on your calendar and treat it like any other non-negotiable appointment. Communicate it with your partner, honour the commitment, and give yourself permission to prioritise your health.

## Creating better sleep habits

Sleep might feel elusive in the early months of parenting—but even small changes can lead to more restorative rest. Think of it not as a rigid goal, but as an evolving practice in care.

1. **Establish a consistent routine**: Going to bed and waking at similar times helps regulate your body's internal clock. It also builds predictability into shared caregiving, easing stress and miscommunication.
2. **Limit stimulants**: Reducing caffeine and alcohol intake in the hours before bed supports more restful, uninterrupted sleep—and makes the next morning feel more manageable.
3. **Create a wind-down ritual**: Reading, meditation, calming music, or low lighting can signal your body and mind that it's time to slow down. These small cues can help you transition more gently into rest.

## Enhancing focus

Sustaining focus in the swirl of parenting, work, and life doesn't happen by accident—it requires intentional habits that honour your priorities and protect your attention. These simple, practical strategies can help realign your focus and create space for presence:

1. **Time-block with purpose**: Carve out specific windows for work, family, and personal wellbeing. When each domain has its place, you reduce overlap, clarify your commitments, and increase your ability to be fully engaged in the moment at hand.
2. **Create a low-distraction zone**: Turn off non-essential notifications. Designate a workspace—whether physical or digital—that signals focus. These small environmental shifts can dramatically reduce cognitive clutter and allow deeper, more sustained attention.
3. **Return to gratitude**: When you feel scattered, pausing to name what you're thankful for can recentre your energy. Gratitude isn't just a feel-good practice—it's a mental lens that helps you refocus on what truly matters.

## The positive ripple effect of wellbeing

When you consistently prioritise exercise, sleep, and focus, the benefits extend far beyond your own wellbeing. These daily choices create a ripple effect that strengthens family dynamics, deepens relationships, and fosters a more supportive environment at home and work.

By modelling healthy habits, fathers quietly influence those around them, especially their children. When your child sees you moving your body, respecting your need for rest, and bringing calm focus to your day, they absorb more than behaviour, they absorb beliefs about what it means to care for oneself.

These seemingly simple acts plant seeds for lifelong practices. They normalise balance. They teach self-respect. And they set the expectation that wellbeing matters—not just for parents, but for everyone in the family system.

When fathers tend to their physical health and mental clarity, they become more emotionally available, and more able to offer presence, perspective, and care. Whether it's listening without distraction, guiding without overwhelm, or reconnecting with a friend or partner, wellbeing fuels connection.

In this way, your investment in yourself becomes a gift to others. Not selfishness but sustainability. Not retreat but reinforcement. A steady foundation that supports love, laughter, and resilience in every corner of your life.

## Positive habits for the future

By maintaining your health and focus, you strengthen your capacity to navigate the challenges of parenting and work with greater resilience. This resilience fuels patience, creativity, and determination, powerful qualities that echo through every corner of family life.

Exercise, sleep, and focus are not luxuries. They are essential foundations of a balanced and fulfilling life. When fathers prioritise these pillars of wellbeing, they enhance their physical strength, emotional steadiness, and mental clarity, equipping themselves to show up fully and effectively at home and at work.

Fatherhood is undeniably demanding but also deeply rewarding. By investing in your own wellbeing, you not only improve your quality of life, but also create a powerful ripple effect: building stronger relationships, modelling healthy behaviours, and creating a home grounded in presence, connection, and care.

Taking care of yourself isn't just for you—it's for your family. Because when you're at your best, you can give them your best.

## Reflective Questions

Take the time to reflect on these questions:

1. What habits or routines help you feel your best (physically, mentally, and emotionally) and how consistent are you with them?
2. Where are you spending energy that drains you, and what could you shift to protect your focus for what matters most?
3. How do you currently recharge and are you giving yourself permission to pause when needed?

# The Next Generation

*"Everything I do now, I know it's shaping how they'll parent one day."*

Fatherhood has evolved from being seen solely as a provider's role to becoming a profound opportunity to shape the future. Today, being a father means far more than ensuring survival and wellbeing. It's an invitation to impart values, nurture resilience, and equip children with the tools they'll need to navigate an increasingly complex world.

Parenting, across generations, has never stood still. It has shifted with social expectations, workplace realities, and the broader cultural landscape. And yet, one hope remains constant: that the next generation will rise higher than the last. That our children will have more opportunities, access better education, enjoy greater wellbeing, and walk forward with strength forged from the lessons we pass down.

This is the great hope of fathers across time and cultures, that through our presence, intention, and effort, our children will soar further. And that in their ascent, they'll carry forward the best of what we've learned and build something even better.

## The role of values in Fatherhood

Our values are shaped by experience, our upbringing, friendships, culture, and even the stories we read or movies we watch. These values form the foundation of our character and decision-making. They guide what we stand for, how we engage with others, and how we move through the world.

Often, values aren't explicitly stated but they can always be felt. You see them in how someone treats others, responds to challenges, or stands up for what matters.

As a father, living your values means modelling authenticity, integrity, and courage. Your child learns not just from what you say, but from how you show up, especially in the quiet moments when no one's watching. Over time, these modelled values become your child's compass, shaping their sense of right and wrong, guiding their relationships, and influencing the choices they make.

That's why it's so important to pause and reflect:

> "What do I stand for?"

> "How consistently do I live those values?"

> "What do I hope to pass on to my child, not just in words but in action?"

Defining and living your values isn't just personal growth, it's an act of legacy. And by doing so, you help raise children who are confident, capable, and courageous in their own right.

## Defining core values

Every family is unique, shaped by its own history, culture, and vision of the future. The values that guide a household are often rooted in personal beliefs, spiritual traditions, and lived experiences. For some families, kindness, empathy, and connection stand at the centre. For others, creativity, responsibility, or a strong work ethic may take focus.

And yet, across generations and cultures, one belief seems to hold steady: a quiet, often unspoken desire to leave the world better than we found it. Fathers model this hope in countless ways through environmental awareness, mindful living, acts of service, or the building of a meaningful legacy. However it's expressed, the intention is the same; to raise children who lead with integrity, courage, and care.

*"I'm not just raising a child—I'm raising someone else's father, partner, friend."*

Defining core values, both individually and with a partner is an intentional act. It invites reflection on your upbringing, the lessons you've carried forward, and the principles you hope to instil in your children. This process can become a shared language within the household like a framework for how you relate, decide, forgive, prioritise, and persevere.

When families know what they stand for, they move through life with more clarity, alignment, and connection. Each member feels a sense of belonging and purpose, not just in the home, but in how they show up in the world.

## Putting your values in action

Children learn far more from what we do than from what we say. Our everyday actions reinforce the importance of values, showing how they play out in real-life situations and helping children internalise them as their own.

For example, a father who values honesty might demonstrate it by openly admitting mistakes and taking responsibility when things don't go as planned. A commitment to compassion could be expressed through acts of service, such as volunteering, checking in on a neighbour, or simply offering a listening ear. These small, consistent acts speak volumes.

Consistency is key. Living your values across different contexts leaves a lasting impression, not just because of what you do, but because you keep showing up the same way, regardless of the setting. Values don't have to be perfectly defined to be powerful. But how you live them through presence, accountability, kindness, or courage, carries weight and shapes your lasting legacy.

Over time, this consistency becomes part of your family's shared rhythm. It reminds your children not just of what matters, but "how" to live with intention. And as they watch you align your actions with your beliefs, they feel inspired and empowered to discover and live their own values.

## Instilling a strong sense of identity

A strong sense of identity gives children a lasting foundation of confidence and self-worth. It helps them understand who they are, where they come from, and what they stand for.

While identity may look different in every household, it is often shaped by cultural, spiritual, and family traditions, each thread weaving a deeper connection to values and heritage. Parents can nurture this by sharing family stories, celebrating cultural milestones, and involving children in meaningful rituals. These practices don't just connect children to the past. They offer grounding in the present, and resilience for the future.

As a father, you have the unique opportunity to shape your child's sense of belonging. Whether it's a regular family dinner, bedtime stories, Sunday hikes, or annual holiday traditions, these moments become emotional landmarks. Ultimately, reassuring your child that they are seen, valued, and a priority in your life.

These simple, consistent practices act as centring points. Even amid the chaos of parenting, work, and the world outside, they remind us of who we are, what we cherish, and how we show up for one another.

## Building resilience in children

Resilience is a vital quality that helps children navigate life's inevitable challenges with strength and adaptability. Fathers who consistently model resilience offer a living blueprint that teaches their children, through actions rather than words, how to meet adversity with courage and composure.

When children witness their fathers navigating setbacks, whether it's recovering from a job loss, managing conflict with calm reasoning, or simply showing up with consistency during difficult times, they absorb something powerful: the understanding that strength isn't about avoiding struggle. It's about meeting it with integrity and grace.

*"I fear the world my kids are growing up in—and whether I'm preparing them enough."*

This modelling takes place in the quiet, everyday moments. Children observe far more than they're told, drawing lasting lessons from how their fathers handle stress, relate to others, and respond when things go wrong. These real-life examples become internal reference points, which build emotional tools they'll reach for when life gets hard.

In an increasingly complex world, a father's example of resilience becomes a gift. One that helps raise confident, capable, and emotionally grounded young people who believe in their ability to adapt, persevere, and keep going.

Resilience isn't a fixed trait, it's an ongoing practice, built moment by moment. For fathers, some of the most powerful lessons in resilience come not through grand gestures, but in the small, everyday choices made under pressure.

When fathers experience inevitable setbacks like challenges at work, financial stress, moments of uncertainty, they can model resilience by speaking openly with their partner and children. Sharing how they're managing disappointment, what they're learning, and how they plan to move forward. These actions send a powerful message: failure isn't final. Growth often emerges through struggle. We are a team.

Resilience also shows up through consistency and self-care. Taking a walk when overwhelmed. Reaching out for support. Maintaining family rituals in the midst of chaos. These practices demonstrate self-respect, emotional regulation, and the belief that tending to your wellbeing is an act of strength, not weakness.

Keeping promises. Staying present. Showing up, even when it's hard. These are the rhythms that build trust and emotional stability. They remind your child that resilience isn't about never bending, it's about being grounded enough to bend and return.

Most importantly, resilience means not shielding children from life's difficulties, but guiding them through with openness, clarity, and steady strength. In doing so, fathers offer their children something profound: the belief that they too can navigate life's uncertainties with courage and care.

## Encouraging problem-solving

One of the most effective ways to build resilience in children is to allow them to face challenges and solve problems independently. While it's often tempting to step in and resolve conflicts or smooth over difficulties, these moments offer rich learning opportunities.

As fathers, we may instinctively reach for solutions but stepping back, even briefly, can create space for our children to try, test, and occasionally fail. These experiences help them reframe challenges not as threats, but as invitations to grow.

Instead of treating mistakes as setbacks, we can ask:

> "What did you learn from that?"

> "What might you try differently next time?"

This simple shift helps children build confidence in their problem-solving abilities and trust in their own inner resources.

Over time, these moments of trial and reflection cultivate self-efficacy, resilience, and a sense of ownership. They prepare children not just to face future challenges, but to meet them with curiosity, creativity, and composure.

## Creating safety in emotions

Emotional intelligence is gaining recognition across schools, workplaces, and families, and at its heart is one essential truth: children thrive when they feel emotionally safe.

Creating that safety doesn't happen by chance. It requires a foundation of trust, built through empathy, kind communication, and patient presence. It's not always about offering solutions. Often, it's about simply being there to sit beside your child in their sadness, frustration, or confusion, and letting them know their emotions are valid.

This kind of presence teaches children that feelings aren't something to fix or fear. They're something to acknowledge, explore, and express. Over time, this builds emotional vocabulary, self-awareness, and a growing confidence in their ability to navigate hard moments.

Equally important is modelling. When fathers manage their own stress with intention, through rest, reflection, or asking for support, they show their children that strong people feel deeply and care for themselves thoughtfully. It reinforces the idea that emotions don't have to be hidden, and that expressing them doesn't alter your love or commitment.

In a world that often rushes past emotion, this kind of steady, compassionate parenting offers something rare and lifelong: the belief that they're safe to be fully themselves, with you.

## Preparing for an unpredictable future

The world our children are growing up in is increasingly complex. Where once our perspective was shaped largely by local or national news, we now live with constant exposure to global events, influenced by politics, climate disruption, civil unrest, and crisis. For many parents, the thought of preparing a child for such an unpredictable future can feel overwhelming.

But amid all that uncertainty lies a powerful truth: our greatest tools are not forecasts or guarantees, they are the values we live, the resilience we model, and the emotional environments we create.

By modelling empathy, courage, adaptability, and emotional steadiness, we lay down foundational tools our children can carry into whatever future unfolds. When children grow in homes that are safe, loving, and principled, they gain something far more powerful than certainty, they gain capacity to endure, adapt and thrive.

Adaptability, in particular, becomes a vital skill. You can nurture this by introducing your child to new environments, whether that's a fresh playground, a cultural event, or a change in daily routine. These small disruptions encourage curiosity, flexibility, and problem-solving.

Just as important is how you navigate your own daily unpredictability. When plans shift or obstacles arise, your response, whether grounded, creative, and open, models how to manage change constructively. Each time you treat an unexpected twist not as a setback but as an opportunity, you help your child build a mindset of resilience and optimism.

In a world you can't always predict, you can prepare a child to face it with courage, care, and adaptability. And that may be the most powerful gift of all.

## Fostering a love of learning

A lifelong love of learning is one of the most powerful gifts a parent can give their child. It shapes not just what they know but how they explore, engage, and grow. At the heart of this love lies curiosity: the innate drive to understand the world and their place in it.

Curiosity is the spark that turns learning into adventure. When children are encouraged to ask questions, like "why the sky is blue", "how bees make honey", or "what happened to the dinosaurs", they begin to see knowledge not as a task, but as discovery. The desire to learn comes from within, and with it comes confidence, creativity, and resilience.

*"Watching them grow into kind, curious humans is the deepest joy I've ever known."*

Encouraging curiosity means making room for wonder. It means slowing down to follow their questions, even when they come at inconvenient moments. It means celebrating not just the answers, but the asking. When we let children follow their "why" questions down unexpected paths, we help them develop not just knowledge, but a mindset of growth, exploration, and joy.

Curiosity is more than a spark. It's the root of a lifelong habit. Children raised in environments where questions are welcomed and exploration is celebrated tend to approach unfamiliar topics with openness, not fear. They become adaptive thinkers, resourceful problem-solvers, and more empathetic interpreters of the world around them.

Curiosity teaches that "not knowing" isn't a shortcoming, it's a starting point. A doorway into discovery.

And when fathers model that same hunger for learning, whether by reading, asking questions aloud, or exploring a new interest, they send a powerful message: learning isn't confined to school or work. It's a way of being in the world. It's how we grow, connect, and contribute.

You can strengthen this love of learning by creating an environment that nurtures exploration:

- Fill your home with books, puzzles, art supplies, and tools for tinkering
- Carve out space for thoughtful conversations and open-ended questions
- Engage in family activities that invite discovery like visiting museums, building things together, or simply watching clouds and naming shapes

These moments don't require elaborate plans. They only ask for presence, wonder, and the willingness to learn side by side.

## Nurturing relationships and community

Children flourish in the context of strong, nurturing relationships and a supportive community. These environments offer emotional safety, belonging, and a sense that they're part of something larger than themselves. As a parent, you help build this foundation by prioritising family time, cultivating meaningful social connections, and instilling values such as empathy, kindness, and cooperation.

These values aren't abstract, they're lived daily. Encouraging your child to consider others' perspectives, and modelling compassion in your own relationships with your partner, friends, and parents, creates a ripple effect of understanding and care.

Acts of service are also powerful tools. Whether it's volunteering as a family, helping a neighbour, or including your child in small kindnesses, these experiences offer concrete lessons in making a difference. When children participate in or witness acts of generosity, they come to see that connection isn't passive, it's something we build through action.

Gratitude deepens this awareness. Simple practices like reflecting each evening on what you're grateful for can help children develop an appreciation for others' contributions and a wider perspective on life. Gratitude and empathy are twin flames, nurturing a child who sees the world not just through their own lens, but with humility and heart.

## Self-reflection and perspective

Self-awareness is a lifelong journey, but its roots take hold in childhood. As children grow, they gradually develop the ability to reflect on their actions, emotions, and emerging sense of identity. Fathers can play a powerful role in nurturing this growth by encouraging their children to explore their values, strengths, and aspirations.

Self-reflection doesn't require grand rituals. It thrives in everyday moments. One-on-one conversations, journaling or drawing, and open-ended questions during family discussions can all foster meaningful insight. Even car rides to school or the shops can become rich spaces for connection. These are the moments that can open the door to deeper understanding, with thoughtful questions like:

- "What was something that made you proud today?"
- "Is there something you're curious about right now?"

Supporting a child's interests is also essential to perspective-building. Whether through creative outlets, sports, or new activities, these experiences allow children to discover what brings them joy and how they want to show up in the world. Pursuing their passions builds not only skills, but confidence, self-knowledge, and a sense of direction.

Ultimately, reflection leads to resilience. When children are invited to think deeply, they begin to understand that their inner world matters. That who they are is worth exploring. And that their evolving story deserves to be told.

## Balancing guidance and independence

Fatherhood has evolved far beyond the traditional image of provider. Today, it encompasses presence, emotional engagement, and a deeper partnership in a child's growth. One of the most meaningful and complex roles of a father is striking the balance between offering guidance and allowing space for independence.

While the instinct to protect your child is both natural and necessary, part of helping them grow is recognising where to step back. This involves creating healthy thresholds for risk like establishing boundaries your child can safely bump against as they learn, explore, and stretch their limits.

It's not about removing challenges, but about building confidence within constraints. Over time, as your child makes decisions, stumbles, and recalibrates, they develop self-trust and trust in you as a steady presence who believes in their ability to grow.

This balance may not come easily at first. But as you observe your child's evolving capabilities, it becomes clearer when to offer a hand and when to simply be nearby as they climb.

Because real independence doesn't come from doing it alone, it grows from being supported to try.

## Encouraging decision-making

Empowering your child to make decisions builds lasting confidence, deepens their sense of self, and strengthens their ability to manage both success and disappointment. By offering decision-making opportunities, especially in everyday moments, you help your child develop the communication and critical thinking skills they'll need throughout life.

Simple choices like picking an afternoon snack, selecting their clothes, or deciding how to spend birthday (or tooth fairy) money, allow children to assert their voice, experience natural consequences, and feel ownership over their choices.

> *"I'm not just raising a kid—I'm shaping someone's future partner, friend, maybe even someone's role model. That keeps me grounded."*

---

Guiding them through this process is key. Helping your child weigh up the pros and cons, talk through outcomes, or reflect on how a choice felt after the fact supports their growing ability to reason and self-regulate. These skills won't emerge all at once but with time, repetition, and encouragement, they form the foundation for thoughtful, resilient decision-making.

As your child matures, gradually increasing the scope of their responsibilities helps them learn to balance freedom with accountability. And your steady presence which provides the reassurance that you're nearby, even when they falter, offers the security they need to keep exploring who they are and how they move through the world.

## Commitment to the next generation

Raising the next generation is one of fatherhood's most profound responsibilities. It is an enduring commitment that calls for intention, patience, and a steady hand. At its heart, this role is about shaping lives through presence, values, and love.

By modelling integrity, encouraging independence, and fostering resilience, fathers offer more than guidance, they offer a living example of how to move through the world with courage and care. Every conversation, boundary, failure, and triumph becomes part of a larger blueprint your child will carry with them.

The journey is rarely straightforward. It's filled with learning curves, emotional whirlwinds, and moments that stretch us beyond what we thought we could hold. And yet, within those moments lie extraordinary opportunities, not only to shape the life of your child, but to ripple outward into the future of communities, workplaces, and society itself.

Because raising a child is never just about them. It's about us. It's about the world we're building, the stories we're telling, and the generations we'll never meet but will feel our influence just the same.

# Reflective Questions

Take the time to reflect on these questions:

1. What kind of person do you hope your child becomes and how are you helping shape that now?
2. What legacy are you building through your words, actions, and presence?
3. What are three values you want your children to remember you for?

# Lessons Learned

*"Fatherhood is not a solo journey—it's shaped by partners, role models, culture, and community."*

Fatherhood is a journey unlike any other. Though it has evolved over time, it remains shaped by challenge, joy, and profound moments of growth from experiences that often redefine who we are. For those who walk this path, the lessons learned don't just inform how we parent, they transform how we see ourselves, our relationships, and the world.

The role you play in your child's life is vital. Through your presence, you shape their understanding of safety, love, and belonging. You build lifetime bonds. You create a legacy of care and guidance that ripples through generations. And the most meaningful parts of fatherhood often aren't found in grand gestures or milestones, but in the small, quiet moments: a bedtime story, a hand held in silence, a laugh shared after a long day.

*Finding Fatherhood* was never meant to be a roadmap. It was a gathering place. A mosaic of insights and reflections from fathers who are still finding their way, who are learning, stumbling, and growing beside their children every day.

There's a saying: "Live the questions now, and perhaps you will then gradually, without noticing it, grow into the answers." That spirit lives here. At the heart *Finding Fatherhood* holds one guiding question: "What do I wish I knew when I first became a father?"

It's a question many fathers carry, especially those working to find their balance in the shifting ground between work, life, and parenting. And while no single answer fits all, this book might be a place to begin. A reflection. A reminder. A gentle hand on the shoulder that says: You're not alone on this journey.

Here is a snapshot of reflections and insights shared throughout *Finding Fatherhood*.

1. **Embracing imperfection:** One of the most universal lessons in fatherhood is letting go of the idea of perfection. Many fathers begin the journey believing they must "get it right" every time. It is a mindset that often leads to stress, doubt, and disappointment. But over time, many come to realise: it's not about being perfect. It's about being present. Mistakes are inevitable, but they create opportunities for growth for you and your child. By embracing imperfection, you model resilience, adaptability, and the courage to keep showing up, even when it's hard.
2. **Learning to apologise:** Embracing imperfection also means learning to take accountability. Parents aren't infallible and admitting when you're wrong builds trust and strengthens relationships. Saying "sorry" when necessary, teaches your child that mistakes don't diminish love. They're moments to model humility, repair, and the truth that love is not based on flawlessness, but honesty and care.
3. **The power of presence:** In an era full of distraction and competing demands, presence is one of the most impactful gifts a father can offer. Being present doesn't require perfection, grand plans, or constant availability. It simply means being here, listening, engaging, and connecting. While your capacity for presence may ebb and flow, thoughtful prioritisation and intentional practices can help you return to

the moment. In doing so, you create the emotional scaffolding your child will carry for a lifetime grounded in safety, trust, and the memory of being truly seen.

## Creating meaningful rituals

Family rituals are more than tradition, they're the heartbeat of connection. Whether it's reading a bedtime story, flipping pancakes on a Sunday morning, or honouring a yearly holiday tradition, these recurring moments weave consistency, joy, and shared identity into a child's world.

Rituals don't have to be elaborate to be meaningful. In fact, their power often lies in their predictability. Creating the comfort of knowing that, no matter what changes outside, this moment is ours. Over time, these rituals become emotional landmarks, grounding children in belonging and giving shape to the rhythm of family life.

Establishing rituals also creates space to disconnect from the noise. Intentionally setting boundaries like "no tech" zones during shared meals or story time, sends a clear message: this moment matters. It allows children to feel the full weight of your attention, reinforcing their sense of importance and security.

These small moments, repeated over time, are not just memories in the making, they are the soil where trust, connection, and love quietly grow.

## Balancing guidance and independence

Many fathers find themselves navigating the delicate balance between providing guidance and allowing space for their child to grow. It's natural to want to protect and steer your child away from harm. That instinct is deeply rooted in love and care.

But fostering independence doesn't mean abandoning guidance. It means offering it with trust and patience. As your relationship deepens, it becomes easier to support your child in taking calculated risks, trying new things, and developing the confidence to make their own decisions.

> *"It's wild to think they'll carry parts of me into the world. I just hope it's the good stuff."*

Children are natural explorers. What they value most is the freedom to test boundaries, learn from experience, and assert their autonomy, all while knowing you are their safe, steady base. Holding onto the knowledge that you are there, close by and loving unconditionally, gives them the courage to step out and grow.

Balancing guidance and independence isn't about getting it perfect every time. It's about returning, again and again, to that quiet promise: I'll support you, and I'll trust you, too.

## Encouraging decision-making

Allowing children to make decisions, even the small everyday ones, lays the foundation for confidence, critical thinking, and resilience. Whether it's choosing what to wear, deciding how to spend pocket money, or navigating friendship dilemmas, these moments give children the chance to explore autonomy and discover what feels right for them.

As a father, one of the ongoing challenges is learning when to step back. There will be times when you can clearly see the missteps ahead but letting your child walk their own path, even when it leads to a stumble, is part of the journey. It's not easy. Watching your child struggle or feel disappointed can tug at every protective instinct you have. But failure, when framed with compassion and reflection, becomes one of life's greatest teachers.

Supporting decision-making means trusting your child's process, offering perspective when invited, and reminding them that mistakes are not a sign of failure but of growth in motion.

Over time, these moments build more than decision-making skills. They shape a child's sense of self, the belief that their choices matter, their voice counts, and their path is theirs to walk, with you walking nearby, always.

## Setting boundaries with love

While fostering independence is essential, children also need boundaries to feel secure. Boundaries offer structure, predictability, and a sense that the world is held together by care, not control.

Many fathers learn, often through experience, how to set expectations in ways that are firm yet deeply loving. In earlier generations, strictness was often seen as the hallmark of good parenting. But today, we understand that effective guidance doesn't require harshness. Rules can be enforced with empathy, clarity, and consistent follow-through.

Setting boundaries with love means explaining the "why" behind the limits. It means including children in discussions about expectations, giving them a voice and a sense of ownership. This collaborative approach nurtures mutual respect and invites children to see boundaries not as punishments, but as expressions of protection, care, and shared understanding.

When children feel heard and when they see that discipline is rooted in love not power, they become more likely to internalise the values behind the rules. And in that trust-filled space, they grow not just obedient, but responsible, reflective, and self-aware.

## Building resilience

Resilience is one of the most enduring gifts a parent can offer. While it can be hard to watch children struggle, these moments often become the most formative. They teach perseverance, resourcefulness, and self-reliance. By offering support without stepping in to solve every problem, parents help their children discover their own strength and develop emotional muscles that will serve them for life.

Resilience is not only taught through strategy, it's transmitted through example. Children learn far more from what they witness than from what they're told. When parents navigate setbacks with perspective, practice self-care, or seek help when needed, they're modelling healthy ways to cope and grow.

*"I want them to grow up kind, strong, and curious. If they do that, I've done my job."*

Over time, these quiet lessons, which are often lived more than just spoken, become a child's internal blueprint. And with it, they gain something truly invaluable: the belief that no matter what life throws their way, they have the tools to face it. Additionally, they hold the steady memory of a parent who lived that truth alongside them.

## The importance of self-care

Parenting is a deeply fulfilling journey but it's also one of relentless responsibility. Many fathers discover, sometimes the hard way, that neglecting their own needs can lead to exhaustion, strained relationships, and emotional disconnection from those they care about most.

Self-care isn't a luxury. It is a form of leadership. It allows you to show up with clarity, calm, and compassion, not just for your children, but for yourself.

What self-care looks like will vary from person to person. For some, it might be a morning run, a weekly yoga session, or carving out time for PlayStation (or whichever platform you prefer). For others, it might mean reading a few quiet pages at night, reconnecting with old friends, or simply sitting in stillness for ten minutes. What matters most is that it replenishes you. That it reminds you who you are, apart from what you do.

When fathers prioritise self-care, they model something essential: that wellbeing matters. It shows that rest is productive. That love also includes the self. And from this restored place, you're better equipped to handle the demands of parenting with patience, perspective, and presence.

## Asking for help

For many fathers, asking for help can feel uncomfortable like admitting weakness or falling short. There's often an unspoken pressure to "have it all together," to solve every problem alone. But the truth is, seeking support is not a sign of failure, it's a recognition that parenting is a journey of learning, growth, and shared responsibility.

---

> *"Some of the best advice I ever got came after saying, 'Mate, I've got no idea what I'm doing.'"*

Asking for help means understanding that you don't have to do it all. It means leaning on your partner, involving family, talking to trusted friends, or reaching out to professionals when needed. These moments of connection can reduce stress, strengthen relationships, and model something powerful for your children: that even adults need support sometimes, and that strength includes vulnerability.

More than anything, asking for help allows you to show up with more presence, patience, and clarity. Because when fathers take care of themselves, they're better equipped to care for those around them.

Help isn't just something you receive. It is something you gain by allowing others in.

## Finding joy in the journey

Parenting is often described as a marathon, not a sprint. This is not just in length, but in spirit. It asks for endurance, patience, and the ability to sustain yourself across years of change, challenge, and growth.

One of the most vital ways to stay grounded through the highs and lows is to find joy in the everyday. Moments of connection like a giggle during bath time, a quiet snuggle on the couch, a shared joke at dinner. These moments can offer the perspective you need when facing sleepless nights, tantrums, or tough days.

Joy is more than just a coping tool; it's a way of seeing. A way of recognising that, amid the messiness, you're witnessing something extraordinary: a small human becoming.

Cultivating joy doesn't mean ignoring the hard parts. It means embracing them with grace, knowing that these are the days you'll one day miss. The spilled cereal, the mismatched socks, the endless bedtime stories, they're all part of the fleeting, precious seasons of your child's life.

And when you pause long enough to see the wonder inside the ordinary, you're reminded of something essential: you're not just raising a child. You're sharing a life. You're shaping a life.

## Celebrating small wins

Parenting often feels like a whirlwind from rushing between school pickups, tantrums, to-do lists, and dinner plans. In the blur, it's easy to focus solely on the big milestones: the first steps, the report cards, the birthdays. But the real beauty of fatherhood often lives in the in-between.

A spontaneous hug.

A curious question asked at bedtime.

A shared laugh over something silly.

The look in your child's eyes when they discover something new.

These small wins, often unnoticed in the moment, are the threads that weave your family's story. They ground you in the present, offering joy, connection, and perspective when days feel long or overwhelming.

Celebrating these moments isn't just about capturing memories. It's about training your heart to notice. Because these are the moments that shape both you and your child and become the stories you'll return to again and again.

## The learning never stops

Parenthood is a journey of constant discovery is shaped as much by trial and error as by wisdom passed down. Along the way, you begin to see that the most meaningful lessons often emerge in the unexpected moments: the missteps, the messy days, the quiet reflections after bedtime, the problem-solving shared with your partner.

By taking time to reflect on your own experiences, you develop a deeper understanding of what truly matters and how to navigate the evolving complexities of raising a child. Each challenge holds a lesson, each joy a reminder of the beauty woven into the everyday.

The road is rarely smooth, but it is rich with opportunity. When you embrace imperfection, prioritise connection, and anchor yourself in presence, you not only grow as a parent, you create something enduring: a legacy of love, resilience, and wisdom.

And perhaps that's the greatest lesson of all: that even as we teach, we are always learning.

# Reflective Questions

Take the time to reflect on these questions:

1. How has your perspective of what it means to be a father changed since beginning *Finding Fatherhood*?
2. What assumptions have you let go of?
3. What areas of your life do you want to show up more fully—as a father, partner, friend, or man?

# An Ongoing Journey

*"Balance isn't static – it's something I have to check in on weekly, sometimes daily."*

Fatherhood is not a destination. It is a lifelong journey, as rewarding as it is demanding. It shifts and reshapes over time, guided by the changing needs of your children, the evolving dynamics of family life, and the drive to grow into your best self.

While each father's path is unique, the journey is marked by shared themes: learning, growth, challenge, and above all: love.

Being a father requires resilience and adaptability. What begins with sleepless nights and bottle feeds gradually transforms into answering big questions, teaching life lessons, and stepping back as your child finds their footing. With each stage comes a new set of responsibilities, and with each challenge, an opportunity to model strength, patience, and presence.

Amid the unpredictability of parenting and the pressures of work, the old archetype of the distant provider has given way to a new one: the engaged father. Today's fathers are not stepping back from responsibility, but stepping forward with intention. They're shaping the narrative, choosing how to show up for their children, their partners, and themselves.

*"My biggest fear? Missing it. Like, being so busy trying to do the right thing that I miss the good stuff."*

Because fatherhood isn't about reaching a fixed destination, it's about walking alongside your child, learning and growing together, one step at a time.

Fatherhood is not a solitary role. It is a deeply collaborative journey, enriched by the shared experiences of families, communities, and generations. Its strength lies not in perfection, but in the willingness to grow alongside your child, to embrace vulnerability, nurture curiosity, and create space where mistakes are welcomed as part of learning.

As children grow, the nature of fatherhood shifts. What begins with leadership gradually becomes companionship. Step by step, you move from guiding to walking beside them, offering support as they grow into their own identities with confidence and clarity.

In that evolving partnership, fatherhood becomes something greater than a list of responsibilities. It becomes a legacy, an enduring imprint of love, strength, and connection that echoes far beyond your own lifetime.

## The journey begins

The transition to fatherhood is a profound moment, marked by anticipation, uncertainty, and a deep sense of responsibility. For many men, it is a transformation that reshapes not only their priorities, but their worldview.

In those early days, everything is new. You're learning not just how to change nappies or soothe a midnight cry, but how to show up for your child, your partner, and yourself. It's a time of great adjustment, requiring patience, humility, and a quiet courage to embrace the unknown.

And while the learning curve can feel steep, it's threaded with moments of wonder: the first time your baby wraps their hand around your finger, the quiet pause between feeds, the realisation that you are now someone's safe place.

These moments don't come with instructions, but they come with meaning. And they mark the beginning of something bigger than fatherhood alone: the lifelong shaping of a legacy, one gentle decision at a time.

*"Honestly, I thought it'd get easier. But it just changes shape. New lessons every week."*

## Being a role model

The responsibilities and challenges of fatherhood inevitably call forward qualities like patience, empathy, and resilience. But beyond these traits lies something even more transformative: the invitation to grow.

Fatherhood often becomes a mirror. Through it, many men come to reflect on their own choices, values, and emotional patterns, redefining what it means to be a man, a partner, and a guide. It's not just about what you teach. It's about how you live.

As a father, your influence isn't limited to big life lessons. It's woven into everyday moments like how you speak to a stranger, how you manage frustration, how you treat your partner, and how you care for yourself. These seemingly small choices echo loudest. Because your child doesn't just listen to your words, they watch your world.

This is the quiet power of modelling. And in choosing to lead with intention, humility, and love, you offer your child something lasting: not the expectation of perfection, but the invitation to live with purpose.

## Commitment to the next generation

As a father, raising the next generation is a profound responsibility that requires intention, patience, and a deep commitment to instilling values and preparing children for life. By modelling integrity, fostering resilience, and encouraging independence, you can guide your children toward becoming compassionate, capable, and confident individuals. While the journey is filled with challenges, steep learning curves and emotional whirlwinds, it is also rich with opportunities to shape not only your child's life but also the future of our communities and society as a whole.

## Strengthening relationships

Parenting can place significant strain on relationships, not just with your partner, but also with close friends, no matter how long you've known them. As priorities shift, time becomes fragmented, often divided between children, work, personal wellbeing, and broader family commitments. This constant juggling act can leave little room for the kind of spontaneous catchups and shared experiences that once sustained friendships.

Over time, you may find yourself at a different life stage than the people around you, some without children, others parenting older kids or walking entirely different paths. The natural reprioritisation that comes with fatherhood can sometimes lead to guilt, disconnection, or even a sense of loss for who you were.

And yet, fatherhood also has the power to deepen connection. Many fathers find that parenting brings a renewed sense of partnership with their significant other, as they navigate the highs and lows together. It can also reshape connections with extended family and old friends, sometimes turning casual relationships into unexpected lifelines of support and solidarity.

*"Since becoming a father, I've realised real friendship isn't about banter—it's about showing up when things get tough and being honest when you're struggling."*

Strengthening relationships during this season often means redefining what connection looks like. It might be shorter conversations, more intention behind fewer interactions, or leaning into new communities aligned with your values and season of life.

Because even as some relationships shift, others deepen. And in that reshaping, you're reminded: change doesn't mean disconnection, it's simply the invitation to connect differently.

## Finding your balance

Fatherhood, as we've explored, comes with its share of challenges. Balancing work, family life, and the emotional and developmental needs of each child can at times feel overwhelming. Yet within these challenges lie opportunities for growth, self-discovery, and deeper connection.

Many fathers grapple with the tension between professional obligations and the desire to be fully present at home. Providing for your family remains important but so does being part of the everyday moments like helping with homework, listening closely, and simply standing by as they fall asleep. This shift represents a powerful evolution from previous generations: a move from presence as provision to presence as engagement.

It's essential to recognise that balance isn't a fixed destination. It's a continuous process of balancing changes with seasons, circumstances, and personal growth.

That process begins with reflecting on your values and priorities, and openly discussing expectations with your partner. These conversations are most effective when grounded in kindness, mutual respect, and a willingness to adapt over time.

From there, build a rhythm that supports your goals and your family's needs. This might include:

- **Setting clear boundaries:** Communicating dedicated work and family time.
- **Establishing meaningful rituals**: Evening walks, screen-free dinners, or weekend adventures.
- **Using time-blocking or planning tools:** Protect time for what matters most.
- **Creating space for recalibration**: Recognising that what works today might evolve tomorrow.

Ultimately, effective parenting isn't about getting every decision right. It's about showing up with intention, again and again.

## Navigating emotional challenges

For generations, boys and men have been shaped by unrealistic expectations. They've been told, often without words, to be stoic, strong, and silent. But today's fathers are rewriting that script. They are choosing to show up with honesty, vulnerability, and the courage to feel.

Fatherhood brings with it a complex range of emotions like feelings of inadequacy, moments of overwhelm, uncertainty about whether you're "doing it right". Navigating difficult conversations with your partner, balancing work stress, and meeting the evolving needs of your children can sometimes leave you feeling like you're walking in the dark.

But you are not alone.

By embracing vulnerability and reaching out to your partner, to other fathers, even to your own father, you open the door to shared understanding. You remind yourself that asking for help, naming your struggles, and being emotionally available aren't signs of failure. They are acts of courage.

---

*"My relationship with my partner changed the day we started seeing each other as teammates—not just parents. Respect, patience, and sharing the load made all the difference."*

---

The old archetype of the strong, silent father may have served a particular time. But today, courage looks different. It looks like empathy, self-awareness, and a willingness to model emotional openness for your children. Because when they see you navigating your inner world with compassion and clarity, they learn that emotions aren't barriers to overcome, they're bridges to connection.

## Love as a driving force

At the heart of fatherhood is love. A love that is unconditional, transformative, and enduring. It's the quiet motor behind sleepless nights, the reason behind hard choices, and the source of joy when your child's eyes light up in wonder. It's a kind of love many fathers describe as unlike anything they've known before, so big, it reshapes your sense of purpose.

This love inspires more than affection. It drives action. It moves fathers to grow, to strive, to show up again and again, even when the tank feels empty. It whispers, be better, not out of obligation, but because you understand how deeply your presence shapes your child's world.

And when challenges arise (as they inevitably do) this love becomes your strength. Whether you're holding a child with a fever through the night, navigating a difficult conversation, or simply hanging on during a long, messy day, love gives you the strength to stay soft in the struggle.

Because in the end, love isn't just what fathers feel. It's how they lead.

## Passing down values

Fatherhood is about more than raising children, it's about leaving a legacy. The lessons you teach, the values you embody, and the love you give create ripples that extend far beyond your own lifetime.

Fathers have a unique opportunity to pass down values that shape a child's character and decisions. Whether it's kindness, integrity, or perseverance, these lessons build the foundation for a meaningful, grounded life.

But values aren't taught through lectures, they're absorbed through living examples. Your child learns not just from what you say, but from what you consistently do. It's in the small acts: the quiet moments shared, the rituals you uphold, the way you handle stress or treat others. These everyday behaviours leave an imprint that they may not fully understand now, but will carry with them for years to come.

Being a present, engaged father helps create shared memories that become a treasured part of your child's inner world. It's not always about how much time you have; it's about the quality of that time. It's your undistracted focus, your willingness to truly see your child, that defines the strength of your bond.

From bedtime stories to Saturday morning pancakes to the simple act of sitting together and talking about your day, these moments weave the fabric of family legacy. They offer comfort, clarity, and a quiet reminder: this is what love looks like in action.

## The endless journey of Fatherhood

Fatherhood is a journey without a final destination. It evolves with each passing year, shaped by the shifting seasons of your child's growth and your own. With every milestone, challenge, and quiet moment, you discover more about who you are and the depths of your capacity for love.

The path isn't always easy. But it is one of the most meaningful journeys a man can take. Fatherhood offers countless opportunities to make a difference, not just in the life of your child, but in the fabric of your family, your community, and the world around you.

Today, fathers are rewriting the script. They're redefining what it means to be present, engaged, and emotionally available not by abandoning their ambition, but by reshaping how they lead at home, in relationships, and at work. This evolution makes space for growth in all directions: professional, personal, and relational.

Navigating this ongoing balancing act requires empathy, communication, and trust. It demands the humility to adapt, the courage to reflect, and the strength to keep showing up with love, even when it's hard.

Ultimately, fatherhood invites you to answer one enduring question: "How do you want to show up for your family, for yourself, and for the world your children will inherit?"

And in that answer lies your legacy.

# A Call to Lead

*"What we model often matters more than what we say—our children watch how we live, not just what we teach."*

Fatherhood is not a finish line; it's a life lived in motion. A quiet revolution of leadership through love.

You may not wear a title. You may never get applause. But every time you show up, every time you listen, every time you choose connection over convenience: you lead.

Leadership through fatherhood isn't loud.

It's not defined by control or perfection.

It's the way you soften when your child cries.

The way you stay when the moment is hard.

The way you say, "I'm sorry," and mean it.

This is the leadership that matters most. The kind measured not by what you accomplish, but by who you become in the eyes of your child.

Let this be your invitation:

- To lead with empathy, not ego
- To model strength through vulnerability
- To craft a legacy through small, consistent acts of care
- To raise your children not by shaping them into something, but by walking beside them as they become someone

You don't have to do it perfectly. You only have to be present.

Because fatherhood isn't just a chapter in your life. It's the story you co-author every day with love as your compass, growth as your rhythm, and leadership as your quiet, enduring gift.

Go well.

# About the Author

Benson Saulo is a father, husband, and first-time author who brings lived experience to the evolving story of modern fatherhood. As a high-performing business leader with a career spanning diplomacy, corporate leadership, and community advocacy, Benson knows firsthand the challenges of balancing ambition with presence at home. *Finding Fatherhood* is born from his personal journey and deep curiosity about how other men are navigating this season of life—with honesty, intention, and love.

www.ingramcontent.com/pod-product-compliance
Lightning Source LLC
LaVergne TN
LVHW041618070426
835507LV00008B/323